LIMPING

CHRISTIANS

HELP FOR THOSE WHO HOBBLE
ALONG THE PATH OF LIFE

JOHN K. LASHELL

Copyright © 2014 John K. LaShell
All rights reserved.
ISBN-13:978-1503010147
ISBN-10:1503010147

DEDICATION
To Grace Community Church,
where these messages were first preached.

MY THANKS
To my wife Heather,
who proofread these chapters, but more
importantly, who believed in the project.

CONTENTS

This small book was originally a series of sermons that flowed from the joining of three separate sources. First, my wife was recovering from a knee replacement and doing a fair bit of limping. Second, I was reading the Banner of Truth edition of *The Bruised Reed*, by Richard Sibbes. As I was meditating on his encouraging counsel to believers who are nearly crushed and whose light is feeble and smoky, I happened to recall a message by D. Martyn Lloyd-Jones included in his *Spiritual Depression: It's Causes and Cure*. That message, "In God's Gymnasium," drew my attention to Hebrews 12:12-13, the text upon which these chapters are based. To the substance of those messages, I have added a few parables—encouragements in story form—for those who see themselves as failures.

One of the things that excites me about preaching is when people leave a service and say, "You must have had me in mind when you were preparing that message." I did not, but God did. It is wonderful and mysterious to see God working to meet the needs of His flock through the preaching of His word. The number of people who responded to these messages was a surprise to me. Perhaps it should not have been. We are all broken and bruised. All of us limp. All of us need healing. God knows that, even if in our pride we sometimes forget it.

A PARABLE:
STUPID STEVIE AND SAINTLY SALLY

Sally and Stevie attend the same church, but they are not part of the same set. They greet one another in church and occasionally exchange a few pleasantries about some banal subject—the weather, the church picnic, or the general depravity of the nation. That's about it.

Sally's set is the Bible-reading, long-praying, bold-witnessing set. She teaches Sunday School, memorizes Scripture, and shows up with her family every time the doors of the church are open. She has a smile for everyone, never becomes angry, and runs her family efficiently. Her children and her husband rise up and call her blessed. Though she pretends not to know it, her friends call her Saintly Sally.

Stevie's set? Well, Stevie doesn't really have a set. Though he always hopes to be included, he is socially ungifted. When he manages to back a conversation partner into a corner, his victim typically glances frantically around, looking for a kind soul who will sacrifice himself by distracting Stevie's attention. It is a vain hope.

Sally has gotten into the habit of mentally referring to him as Stupid Stevie. His lack of social grace carries over into the workplace, which has cost him several jobs. Stupid Stevie. When he gets a little money, he spends it because he deserves a vacation or a new toy. Therefore, his family is always dangling over the brink of insolvency. No one at church can understand how they manage to hang on. Stupid Stevie.

At home, Stevie insists on being the center of attention. Fortunately, he is not a violent man, but he exercises his power in other ways. He says "no" to his wife and children at every opportunity because it feeds his ego. He has never learned the power of "yes." Stevie complains endlessly that he doesn't receive the respect he deserves. If he would listen, the folk at church would like to tell him that he has not earned the respect of his family. Stupid Stevie.

Sally sometimes wonders what kind of place Stevie could ever fill in heaven. "Maybe the Lord will assign him the task of cleaning the toilets," she says to herself with a chuckle. "I think he might manage that if the toilets in heaven never get dirty."

How does Stevie see his relationship to God? His connection to the Lord feels like a greased grapevine. He swings through the jungle of life always just a few feet above the hungry lions. Hand over hand, hand over hand—Stevie tries to climb up to Jesus. He believes in Jesus. He wants to be near Jesus, but whenever he makes a bit of progress, fate squirts a little more grease on the grapevine and down he slides. His great fear is that he will reach the end of the vine, his faith will fail, and the prowling beasts below will tear him limb from limb. He does not know that underneath him are the everlasting arms. He does not recognize the many times those arms have lifted him up, and His Father has whispered, "Your faith shall not fail."

One day, the angel of death came calling, first at Sally's house, and then at Stevie's.

Sally lay on a clean white sheet under a flowered coverlet. Her family were ringed around her bedside absorbing her final blessings—a word of hope and confidence for each one. At last she said, "I think I'll be going now," and she closed her eyes. When she opened them again, it seemed that her bed had become an open boat garlanded with blossoms and guided by a shining being across the wide river of death. On the other shore, glorious angels greeted her with shouts of joy and conducted her to the throne room of the King of kings.

"Welcome to My home. It is good to have you here, my child," He said. Awestruck by His beauty, Sally said nothing.

"You have served me long and diligently, Sally. My angels will conduct you to a changing room. There you will find your new garments and the accessories, which are your reward. Do not tarry long because someone you know will be arriving shortly."

A few minutes later, Sally reappeared, robed in white with a golden circlet around her forehead. Jewels sparkled in her in her hair and on her crown. Her robe was trimmed with golden braid. Sapphire earrings and a matching sapphire necklace set off her blue eyes to perfection. She was very pretty. She knew it, and she was very pleased.

As she stepped out of the changing room, she followed the watching eyes of the assembled heavenly beings. There, up in the air, a long way off flew a shining angel carrying a wriggling, flopping bundle. What was it?

The bundle was Stevie. On the last day of his earthly life, Stevie felt himself inexorably slipping down his grapevine. The hungry beasts were growling below, but he no longer had the strength to struggle back up out of their reach. He wailed. He cried. He begged for mercy, "Pease, Lord, just one more day, just one more hour." Then he came to the end, and he fell. The lion looked up and opened his mouth in greedy anticipation, but just then a strong hand latched on to the back of Stevie's nightshirt and bore him off into the heavens.

After a few seconds, Stevie gathered up enough breath and enough courage to look back over his shoulder. The shining face of the angel was too bright for him to bear, so he looked away, back down toward the rapidly receding earth. "Who are you?" he managed to croak.

"I am the angel of death."

"I thought you were supposed to be dark, ugly, and holding a sharp sickle," said Stevie.

"I appear in that guise to some people, but never to the beloved ones. Here we are. You are home."

With that, the angel swooped past the gates, towers, and walls and deposited Stevie on the floor in front of the King's throne. He landed on his hands and knees with an awkward thump. "Stupid Stevie," thought Sally. "He can't even enter heaven in a proper fashion."

After Stevie had managed to scramble to his feet, the King said, "Welcome. It is very good to have you here, my child."

"Am I . . . am I actually in heaven? Are you going to let me stay?"

"Yes, indeed. You belong to Me. This is My home, and where I am, there you are to stay for all eternity."

"But I have been so bad. I've made a mess of my life. I haven't done anything for You, as Sally has. She deserves to be here, but I don't."

"No one deserves to be here, My child. I have forgiven all your past because you believed that I died for sinners and rose again. I was your only hope and you clung to me. Many times when you were about to fall into the lion's mouth I lifted you up. I kept you, and I have brought you home."

Stevie's eyes shone with adoration and wonder. "You are amazing, Lord! I love You. I love You. I love You."

At that moment, there was such an explosion of light that Sally had to close her eyes. When she opened them again she saw Stevie, but what a change had come over him! He was robed in white so brilliant that she could hardly bear to look at him. He had not a single reward of gold or gem, but he was standing much nearer the throne than she. Sally looked down at her own gown. It was still white, but his shone like the sun.

She looked up at her Lord, and He answered the question in her face that she dared not utter.

"Did you not know that closeness to Me in heaven depends not on what you have accomplished, but on how much you love Me? Some have done great deeds out of a small love, and they shall receive a small reward. Others have done small deeds, according to their ability, out of a great love, and they shall receive a great reward.

"The great deed of some exceedingly weak ones is that they kept clinging with their feeble faith to Me. When at last they come into My presence and see how I have upheld them, their hearts fairly burst with love. He who is forgiven little loves little. He who is forgiven much loves much. So Stevie is here close to Me."

"Oh, my Lord," cried Sally. "In my heart I have despised this one that You love, and with my mouth I have made many a snide remark to my friends about this glorious son of Yours. I even called him 'Stupid Stevie' when the angel dropped him down before Your throne. I never saw the wickedness of my heart as I see it now. Can you ever forgive me? Can Stevie ever forgive me?"

Sally bowed her head and tears began to fall in a little pool at her feet. God's shining son, Stevie, turned around, came toward Sally, and put an arm around her shoulders. "Of course, I forgive you Sally. I have always admired you. I used to think you were wonderful, and I still do."

Suddenly, a blinding light flashed out from Him who sat on the throne. Sally closed her eyes briefly. When she opened them again, she and Stevie were standing side by side close to the throne. She looked down at her gown and saw that it was gleaming white, as bright as the sun.

And so the first shall be last, and the last shall be first.

HEBREWS 12:1-15

Therefore, since we have so great a cloud of witnesses surrounding us, let us also lay aside every encumbrance and the sin which so easily entangles us, and let us run with endurance the race that is set before us, fixing our eyes on Jesus, the author and perfecter of faith, who for the joy set before Him endured the cross, despising the shame, and has sat down at the right hand of the throne of God. For consider Him who has endured such hostility by sinners against Himself, so that you will not grow weary and lose heart. You have not yet resisted to the point of shedding blood in your striving against sin; and you have forgotten the exhortation which is addressed to you as sons, "My son, do not regard lightly the discipline of the Lord, nor faint when you are reproved by Him; for those whom the Lord loves He disciplines, and He scourges every son whom He receives." It is for discipline that you endure; God deals with you as with sons; for what son is there whom his father does not discipline? But if you are without discipline, of which all have become partakers, then you are illegitimate children and not sons. Furthermore, we had earthly fathers to discipline us, and we respected them; shall we not much rather be subject to the Father of spirits, and live? For they disciplined us for a short time as seemed best to them, but He disciplines us for our good, so that we may share His holiness. All discipline for the moment seems not to be joyful, but sorrowful; yet to those who have been trained by it, afterwards it yields the peaceful fruit of righteousness. Therefore, strengthen the hands that are weak and the knees that are feeble, and make straight paths for your feet, so that the limb which is lame may not be put out of joint, but rather be healed. Pursue peace with all men, and the sanctification without which no one will see the Lord. See to it that no one comes short of the grace of God; that no root of bitterness springing up causes trouble, and by it many be defiled.

CHAPTER 1
LIMPING CHRISTIANS

We want the Christian life to be easy and comfortable. It is not. We think that if our Father loves us, He should give us all pleasant things and shelter us from all painful things. He does not. Instead, we read that "He disciplines us for our good," and that "All discipline for the moment seems not to be joyful, but sorrowful" (Hebrews 12:10-11).

Part of His discipline is to have us exercise our painful joints and limbs. As anyone going through physical therapy can tell you, that hurts. "Therefore, strengthen the hands that are weak and the knees that are feeble, and make straight paths for your feet, so that the limb which is lame may not be put out of joint, but rather be healed" (Hebrews 12:12-13). This exhortation seems contrary to the command with which the chapter begins: "Run with endurance the race that is set before us" (v. 1). We are supposed to run, but the text then addresses us as people who can barely hobble.

We want to run, but we must first be cured of our painfully lame condition. What causes us to limp along in our lives as Christians, and is there any hope for improvement?

Causes of a spiritual limp

Distractions, injuries, and poor technique can make the difference between winning and losing a race. Hebrews 12 suggests several things that may hinder us from pressing on "toward the goal for the prize of the upward call of God in Christ Jesus" (Philippians 3:14).

We may be limping because of awkward burdens. If we are to run well, we must "lay aside every encumbrance" (Hebrews 12:1). The word encumbrance refers to burdens that may be heavy, but are mostly just awkward. They are things that impede progress and movement. We can't run well carrying a card table, even if it isn't that heavy. These encumbrances or awkward burdens represent things in our lives that hold us back. They keep us from following the Lord Jesus with a whole heart.

Many a young person has been hindered from going all out for Jesus by older people who say, "Don't take this religious business to extremes. You need to watch out for yourself. You don't want to become a fanatic. It's fine for you go to church because it makes you feel better, but don't get carried away. I had a religious phase when I was young, but it passed, and I expect your excitement will cool off in time too." I remember hearing that kind of discouraging advice when I was a teen. The thing that helped me then was looking at the older men and women of God in my church who still loved and served the Lord with all their heart. If their passion for Christ had not cooled, perhaps I could ignore the wisdom of the world.

Another encumbrance may come from good friends who don't care about the Lord. They are not openly hostile to Him; they are not exceptionally wicked, but when you are with them, you find yourself thinking and caring less about Jesus. The standard argument for retaining such friends is that Jesus ate with tax collectors and sinners. If Christians have no outside friends, they will never have an opportunity to win people to Christ. That is, of course, true, but might there be a difference between Jesus and you? When He was with the outcasts of society, He raised them up. When you are with worldly friends, do they pull you down? If your friendship with unsaved people leads them to serious thoughts and spiritual conversations, that is well and good. If your friends cause you to think, speak, and act in ways that you would be ashamed to acknowledge to your pastor, they are an awkward burden that needs to be laid aside.

A third kind of awkward burden that may hinder us from running well is the thing we hold dear, the thing we do not want to share or lose. It may be our time—we have precious little of it for ourselves. It may be our homes—we don't want them messed or our privacy disturbed. It may be money that we love to spend or money that we love to hoard. Perhaps what we hold dear is our reputation with the "in" group at work, and we will not risk it to befriend the friendless.

There are, of course, too many kinds of encumbrances to list them all. The crucial question you and I must face is this: am I lugging something about that cools my love for the Lord Jesus?

We may be limping because of entangling sins. The author of Hebrews exhorts us to "lay aside.... the sin which so easily entangles us" (12:1). The image that comes to my mind is the time when our friend's dog wrapped his leash around his mistress's ankles and caused her to stumble and fall down. Her broken arm limited her activities for a few months. Sin can tangle us up and keep us from running the race. When it trips us up, we might sprain an ankle or break a leg. Then we truly are lame.

I am encouraged that this verse treats entangling sin as a common problem. The writer includes himself, for he says "us," and he notes that it catches hold of us easily. These entangling sins are not the sudden, unexpected attacks of the devil that seem to come out of nowhere. They are the struggles every Christian endures every day of his life. The apostle Paul expressed this for all of us when he wrote,

> *For I know that nothing good dwells in me, that is, in my flesh; for the willing is present in me, but the doing of the good is not. For the good that I want, I do not do, but I practice the very evil that I do not want. But if I am doing the very thing I do not want, I am no longer the one doing it, but sin which dwells in me. I find then the principle that evil is present in me, the one who wants to do good. For I joyfully concur with the law of God in the inner man, but I see a different law in the members of my body, waging war against the law of my mind and making me a prisoner of the law of sin which is in my members. Wretched man that I am! Who will set me free from the body of this death (Romans 7:18-24)?*

Many Christians do not understand this struggle at all. They think that victory over sin ought to come easily. After all, they have been saved by the blood of Christ from the guilt and penalty of sin. They have the indwelling Holy Spirit who has broken the power of sin—or has He? Their struggles with sin leave them puzzled and confused. "Am I really a Christian after all?" they wonder. I can remember having such doubts when I was a teen.

Contrary to some Christian preaching, all sins are not created equal. If a fellow is a hit man for the Mafia, or if he casts magical curses on his enemies, or if he is pimping for a couple of prostitutes, he is not a Christian troubled by entangling sins. This man is bound for hell.

Many Christians struggle with anger, lust, or jealousy, or they have horrible blasphemous thoughts popping into their heads. They hate these thoughts. They long to be free of them. These are the kinds of sins the apostle is describing in Romans 7.

The thing that trips believers up is often not the sin itself, but their false notion that true Christians do not deal with such thoughts and habits. To the contrary, the Bible paints a very dark picture of our human nature. When we are saved, that darkness is still in us. The Holy Spirit brings the light of God into our souls, and He pushes the darkness back to some degree, but like black oily smoke, the darkness keeps seeping out and contending with the light. Before conversion and before the Holy Spirit comes in, we do not notice the darkness. His light is what makes us more aware of the dark corners of our hearts, and that awareness is a good thing.

I do not mean that Christians should excuse or make light of their besetting sins. We need to fight against them by the power of the Holy Spirit (Romans 8:12-13). On the other hand, we must always remember that the blood of Jesus cleanses us from all sin and makes us acceptable in the sight of God. Do not give in to despair when sin entangles you and trips you up. Get up and keep on fighting.

We may be limping because we are fainting under lengthy trials. "You have forgotten the exhortation which is addressed to you as sons, 'My son, do not regard lightly the discipline of the Lord, nor faint when you are reproved by Him'" (Hebrews 12:5). Most of us can manage fairly well when we face minor, short-term obstacles. However, when difficulties go on and on, and when we cannot see how to solve them, then we are apt to become discouraged and to faint under our burdens.

This word *faint* is an interesting one. It carries the idea of losing your grip on something because you are exhausted. You just can't hold on to the edge of the cliff any longer, so you finally let go. After her knee-replacement surgery, Heather had several episodes of feeling faint. She didn't lose consciousness, but she felt weak and woozy when she sat up. In the spiritual sense, this fainting is likely to happen when troubles pile up and refuse to go away. We become overwhelmed, discouraged, and anxious. This is a common condition, so the author of Hebrews found it prudent to warn us about it.

Some Christians are more prone to feeling faint than others. Here again, the problem sometimes lies with the guilt that hounds them, rather than with the pressures that pile up on them. They say, "If I were a good Christian, I would not become anxious and depressed. I should be able to overcome these feelings. I pray and I ask God for help, but still I struggle. Therefore, I am a bad Christian, and I might as well give up."

There are, of course, many different causes for fainting under life's burdens. Sometimes there are physical problems, perhaps a genetic tendency toward anxiety, or a hormonal imbalance. Sometimes external tragedies and trials pile up like 300-pound tackles on a downed receiver. Sometimes doctrinal errors cause people to view life in the wrong way. They think that only great sinners have great trials.

Whatever the cause, when we become faint, we limp along through life instead of running the race.

Finally, we may be limping if we are embittered by deep hurts. "See to it that no one comes short of the grace of God; that no root of bitterness springing up causes trouble, and by it many be defiled" (Hebrews 12:15).

Bitterness is far more damaging to the soul than awkward burdens, persistently entangling sins, or lengthy trials. You feel you have been wronged, and maybe that is true. You feel justified in harboring angry, spiteful thoughts. You would like to get even, but you don't dare. If your enemy had a great fall, you might show some outward sympathy, but inwardly you would feel a little leap of happiness in your heart, and you would say, "It serves him right." Perhaps you are even bitter toward God because He has not met your expectations, so, like a pouting child, you have turned your back on Him.

Bitterness is very common, even among Christians. Our text says that by it *many* are *defiled*. Hebrews 12 does not say the other things that cause Christians to limp defile them, so bitterness must be especially dangerous. Bitterness defiles believers as a dye or stain impregnates the fibers of cloth. It imparts a foul color (and odor) to the soul. Think of a baby's diaper. Bitterness steals peace from the heart; it makes us unpleasant company; and most importantly, it causes God to turn away His face. You cannot be happy in Jesus when you are hateful toward those who have hurt you.

Like an unwelcome tenant in a rented property, when bitterness inhabits the heart, it defends its right to stay with an appeal to the law. "Justice has not been done," it says, "and therefore I must keep pressing my case forward." Bitterness in the heart does not like to surrender its rights to God, so we must fight it with the words of Scripture: "Never take your own revenge, beloved, but leave room for the wrath of God, for it is written, 'Vengeance is Mine, I will repay, says the Lord'" (Romans 12:19).

Beloved brother or sister in Christ, you may think your enemies are the people who take away your rights or who threaten your person and your prosperity. Bitterness is a far greater foe than these. By the power of the Holy Spirit, hate and fight this threat to your soul more fiercely than you would any outward enemy. See to it that bitterness does not take root in your heart and by springing up defile you.

Encouragement when we are limping

Hebrews 12 not only describes the causes of a lame and limping condition. It also encourages us to keep moving when we are so tired of stumbling along that all we want to do is to sit down and give up.

Take courage from the example of your Savior. Fix your eyes on Jesus

> *. . . the author and perfecter of faith, who for the joy set before Him endured the cross, despising the shame, and has sat down at the right hand of the throne of God. For consider Him who has endured such hostility by sinners against Himself, so that you will not grow weary and lose heart. You have not yet resisted to the point of shedding blood in your striving against sin (Hebrews 12:2-4).*

Why does this text tell us to fix our eyes on Jesus? The Lord wants us to remember and meditate on several truths about our Savior. First, think of the terrible sufferings of Christ on the cross. He endured horrible physical pain. He endured the mockery and laughter of His ene- mies. He bore the awful wrath of God that pressed down on His pure and innocent soul. When you are limping along, take your eyes off yourself for a while and meditate on the sufferings of Christ. That is an excellent remedy for the attractions of sin or the temptation to give up.

Next, remind yourself that your trials and troubles are infinitely less than what Jesus suffered. Certainly, you are very vexed and worn down by what you must face. I do not want to minimize that, but He endured an ocean of suffering for you. You were drowning in your sins and sorrows, but Jesus dove into them and pushed you into the shallow water near the shore. Now the waves may come up to your neck, but they won't go over your nose (Isaiah 43:2). He has turned your ocean into a puddle.

Finally, think of the joy that Christ kept before His eyes. He kept thinking about how pleased the Father would be once the pains of the cross were all over. He looked ahead to the marriage supper of the Lamb and to feasting at that heavenly table with all the people He was redeeming by His death. That, too, is an excellent remedy for temptation and trials and bitterness. Keep your eyes fixed on the glory you will share with Jesus when this is all over.

Take courage from the love of your Father.

For those whom the Lord loves he disciplines, and He scourges every son whom He receives. It is for discipline that you endure;

God deals with you as with sons; for what son is there whom his father does not discipline? But if you are without discipline, of which all have become partakers, then you are illegitimate children and not sons. Furthermore, we had earthly fathers to discipline us, and we respected them; shall we not much rather be subject to the Father of spirits, and live (Hebrews 12:6-9)?

When you are down and discouraged, defeated, and depressed, do not think that God is against you. Do not conclude that He has turned His back on you. He loves you more than any earthly father ever loved his child. He loves you more than any earthly mother loved the babe in her arms. You may not see His smiling face. Perhaps you even think you see a frown. No matter what happens to you, the weight of His love for you has not decreased by as much as goose-down feather because He loved you before you were born. He loved you before He created the heavens and the earth. He has loved you with an everlasting love (Jeremiah 31:3).

In the middle chapters of Isaiah, we see the nation of Israel, tried, tested, and troubled. The people, feeling rejected and dejected, cry out, "The LORD has forsaken me, and the Lord has forgotten me." Then the Lord responds, "Can a woman forget her nursing child and have no compassion on the son of her womb? Even these may forget, but I will not forget you" (Isaiah 49:14-15). At the cross, God the Father turned His back on His only begotten Son so that you and I who trust in Him will never need to cry out, "My God, my God, why have You forsaken me?"

I doubt that my children felt loved when I was punishing them. I am sure I did not feel loved when my mother thrust me outside to perform the annual weeding of the geranium bed in our front yard. Nevertheless, in both cases love—unwavering love—was surely present.

Take courage from the goal of your discipline. God could end your suffering now. He could remove your temptations and your entangling sins in an instant. He could relieve you of your awkward encumbrances so that you would be able to run the race with a light and happy heart. He has not chosen to do that either for you or for me. Why? What is He aiming at? The answer is very simple. He wants us to be holy as He is holy.

> *As obedient children, do not be conformed to the former lusts which were yours in your ignorance, but like the Holy One who called you, be holy yourselves also in all your*

behavior; because it is written, "You shall be holy, for I am holy" (1 Peter 1:14-16).

This creates a problem for us, because we are often disobedient and unholy. So what does a good father do in order to train disobedient children?

For they disciplined us for a short time as seemed best to them, but He disciplines us for our good, so that we may share His holiness. All discipline for the moment seems not to be joyful, but sorrowful; yet to those who have been trained by it, afterwards it yields the peaceful fruit of righteousness (Hebrews 12:10-11).

Now this is a wonderful passage. We do not need to produce our own holiness by some heroic acts of dedication. God our Father plans to give us greater and greater measures of His own holiness. All of the things that make you limp, all the painful things God has not taken away, all the things you long to be rid of—He has a purpose for them. He wants to give you more of Himself because He cannot separate His holiness from Himself. All of the things that you count as great evils are goads, pointed sticks to prod you toward your Father. The more helpless and hopeless you see yourself to be, the more you will cry out to Him for help. The weaker you are, the more you will depend on His strong arm. Your loving heavenly Father leaves some inward corruptions and permits some outward trials to teach you to lean on Him and Him alone.

Holiness is not our victory over sin. Holiness is being filled with the Holy Spirit. Holiness is being drawn into the life of God. Holiness only grows in us as we flee from our sins, our weaknesses, and our burdens to rest in the Lord Jesus Christ and our Father.

Trials, temptations, and troubles are not an automatic pathway to holiness. We may waste them if we "regard lightly the discipline of the Lord" (Hebrews 12:5). If we simply say, "Into every life a little rain must fall," and if we fail to see our Father's purpose, then we will derive no benefit from the hard things of life. Our Father "disciplines us for our good, so that we may share His holiness."

One last thought: If you are currently limping along, the Lord Jesus understands and sympathizes with your weakness (Hebrews 4:14-16). Even if you limp all the way to heaven, He will still let you in and greet you with a hug and with the song of the angels. On the other hand, He wants you to become stronger. If you seek Him, He will help you on toward greater health.

A PARABLE: REMEMBER THE DUCK

In November 1983, I wrote a brief parable for a sermon on Psalm 103. I still have the hand-written notes for that message. Someone must have heard it on a tape, or perhaps I wrote it out several years later in an email. Somehow, this simple story has been copied all over the Internet. Occasionally the names or a few details have been changed. I even found a Muslim version using the names Ahmed and Fatima, and someone included it in a book he published. Usually, it is listed as anonymous, though a few who posted it have agreed to note me as the author. Here it is, with a few changes of my own.

Billy and Suzie were staying at their Grand-parents for the summer. Billy had a new slingshot. He aimed at posts, and boulders, and cans. He almost never hit anything. One after-noon as his grandmother's favorite duck waddled by, Billy let fly a stone. This time his aim was true, and the duck fell dead. He looked fearfully around, and seeing no one, he carried the dead duck into the woods and buried it under some leaves, sticks, and stones. When he turned around, his sister was standing at the edge of the woods, watching him. Not a word passed between them.

Later that afternoon, Grandpa said, "How would you two like to go to town with me. I need some things from the hardware store, and I thought we could stop for an ice-cream cone. Grandma said, "Billy can go, but I need Susie to help with supper tonight."

Suzie piped up, "Oh, I think Billy wanted to help you tonight, didn't you Billy?" Then, in a whisper. with her back to her grandma, she added, "Remember the duck!" So Billy stayed and helped with supper. Billy also washed the dishes in Suzie's place, and he took out the trash. In fact, for the next three days, he did every one of Suzie's chores. All she had to do was to whisper, "Remember the duck. Remember the duck. Remember the duck."

Finally, Billy couldn't stand it any longer. With shame, fear, and tears he told his Grandma what he had done. She wrapped her arms around him and said, "I saw everything out the kitchen window. I've already forgiven you because I love you. I wondered how long you would let Susie make a slave out of you."

And that is what God says to us. "I know what you have done. I have already forgiven you because I love you. Why do you allow the devil to make you a slave to your guilt and your fear. Don't you believe in My grace? Don't you believe that My Son has made you free?"

CHAPTER 2
LIMPING CHRISTIANS
AND LAME DUCKS

A lame duck can't keep up with the rest of the flock, so it is easy prey for a fox or a coyote. In political terms, lame ducks are elected officials who are on their way out of office. They have lost an election, and they are about to be replaced, but before they go, they are still able to do a little damage to the body politic.

Sometimes limping Christians wonder if they are really saved. They wonder if they are lame ducks after all. Maybe they haven't been elected by God, and they will soon be kicked out of the kingdom. These are the people I want to comfort and encourage in this chapter.

In Mark 9, a frantic father brought his demon-possessed son to the disciples of Jesus. When they were not able to help the boy, the father appealed to the Lord.

"It has often thrown him both into the fire and into the water to destroy him. But if You can do anything, take pity on us and help us!" And Jesus said to him, "'If You can?' All things are possible to him who believes." Immediately the boy's father cried out and

said, "I do believe; help my unbelief" (vv. 22-24).

"I do believe; help my unbelief!" He had a weak faith, but it was a genuine faith, and his weak faith was enough for Jesus to heal his son. A weak, limping faith in Christ still leads to salvation.

A limping Christian's faith differs in several important respects from the faith of lame ducks. By considering these differences carefully, a limping Christian may be assured that he will not be caught by the fox or cast out of office.

Limping Christians differ from lame ducks in their attitude toward sin.

A person's attitude toward his sins is one of the best indicators of his spiritual condition. Here we see a marked difference between true, though weak, Christians, and bold hypocrites.

Lame ducks frequently sin with a cheerful confidence. There is a proper confidence that God's children should have, but there is also such a thing as a presumptuous, misplaced, sinful confidence. Many lame ducks are confident of their salvation. They sin boldly. They are sure that God will forgive them, so they are not concerned about judgment. We see this attitude in two of the letters that Jesus sent to His churches in Asia minor—modern Turkey.

Jesus threatened to discipline the church at Pergamum

> *... because you have there some who hold the teaching of Balaam, who kept teaching Balak to put a stumbling block before the sons of Israel, to eat things sacrificed to idols and to commit acts of immorality (Revelation 2:14).*

He similarly accused the church at Thyatira:

> *I have this against you, that you tolerate the woman Jezebel, who calls herself a prophetess, and she teaches and leads My bond-servants astray so that they commit acts of immorality and eat things sacrificed to idols. I gave her time to repent, and she does not want to repent of her immorality (vv. 20-21).*

A loose attitude toward sexual immorality was not just a problem in these early churches. It keeps cropping up. Several years ago, I knew a pastor who had formerly been a youth minister. A girl in his youth group frequently stood up to give warm, glowing testimonies about the grace of Christ. Eventually, several of the teens approached my friend and said to him, "We can't stand it any longer. You should know that this girl is the most immoral girl in our high school. She will sleep with just about anybody." When my friend confronted her with this accusation, she replied, "Well, the Lord forgives, doesn't He? That's what He's there for."

Lame ducks often think that God does not really care about their sin. They turn the grace of God into an excuse to do whatever they please without fear. They do not know that the fox is hiding just around the next bush, and their days are numbered.

Limping Christians have a sensitive conscience regarding their sins. A limping Christian wants to obey God. He is careful to avoid things that he knows will displease the Lord. He looks at the corruptions of his heart, and he is grieved. He fights against his sins and seeks to subdue them by the power of the Holy Spirit.

Part two of *Pilgrim's Progress* by John Bunyan introduces us to a number of limping Christians: Master Fearing, Master Feeble-mind, Master Ready-to-halt, Master Despondency and his daughter Much-afraid. They need constant support from their guide, Great-Heart. Master Fearing, for example, was always in doubt about whether he would be accepted by the Lord Jesus. Throughout his journey toward the heavenly city, he faced outward difficulty bravely. On the other hand, he "dreaded sin and coming short of Heaven, more than all that flesh could do unto him. He was alarmed more at the fear of being overcome by temptation, than from a reluctance to undergo derision or persecution."[1] Outward problems did not shake his assurance of salvation, but his inward temptations and failures did.

Limping Christians and lame ducks differ in their attitude toward their sins. If you are comfortable with your transgressions of God's law and confident that you can keep all your sins and still go to heaven, beware lest you discover that you are a lame duck who has not been elected to fill the seat of a true Christian. Limping Christians are not like that. They have a sensitive conscience.

Limping Christians differ from lame ducks in the object of their trust.

The only way to be saved is to trust in Jesus Christ. He died to pay the penalty for our sins. He rose to give us divine life. He seals us with His Holy Spirit, who keeps us safe all the way to glory. That is the reason limping Christians do

---

[1] *John Bunyan, Pilgrim's Progress from This Word to That Which Is to Come, the Second Part,* PDF Kindle edition, (London: Printed for Nathanael Ponder, 1684), 210, editor's note 65.

not fall prey to the foxy devil, as lame ducks do. They are not stronger than the ducks, but they are "protected by the power of God through faith for a salvation ready to be revealed in the last time" (1 Peter 1:5). Jesus Christ and He alone must be the object of our trust or we will not make it all the way to glory.

Instead of trusting in of Christ, lame ducks may trust in their own excellence. A certain kind of person is self-deceived about his own goodness. He is the opposite of the man who sins with bold confidence in his salvation. To the contrary, he thinks that he is morally excellent. He doesn't see any sin in himself. He may insist (as I have heard one man say), "I'm too busy doing good things to sin."

Jesus described this kind of person in His parable of the Pharisee and the tax collector.

And He also told this parable to some people who trusted in themselves that they were righteous, and viewed others with contempt: "Two men went up into the temple to pray, one a Pharisee and the other a tax collector. The Pharisee stood and was praying this to himself: 'God, I thank You that I am not like other people: swindlers, unjust, adulterers, or even like this tax collector. I fast twice a week; I pay tithes of all that I get.' But the tax collector, standing some distance away, was even unwilling to lift up his eyes to heaven, but was beating his breast, saying, 'God, be merciful to me, the sinner!' I tell you, this man went to his house justified rather than the other; for everyone who exalts himself will be humbled, but he who humbles himself will be exalted" (Luke 18:9-14).

It is hard to lead a Pharisee into the kingdom of heaven because he has such a high opinion of himself. As a very tall person is apt to bang his head against the lintel of a door, so a proud person, who refuses to stoop, knocks himself out at heaven's doorway. Only the lowly may enter there.

Instead of trusting in Christ, lame ducks may trust in their own experiences. Religious experiences of one kind or another are more widespread among ordinary people than is generally realized. Visions, voices, dreams, spiritual impressions, bodily spasms, and automatic writing that seems to come straight from God through the fingers without going through the brain—all of these are more or less common. Unless they are familiar with the psychology of religious phenomena, most people who experience such things are confident that they have received a direct visitation from the Lord. Some of these are surely demonic, but probably many more are simply products of the individual's psyche. Whatever the source, Scripture warns us about trusting in them.

> *Let no one keep defrauding you of your prize by delighting in self-abasement and the worship of the angels, taking his stand on visions he has seen, inflated without cause by his fleshly mind, and not holding fast to the head, from whom the entire body, being supplied and held together by the joints and ligaments, grows with a growth which is from God (Colossians 2:18-19).*

I remember a man in Wisconsin who liked to talk about the time when Jesus Christ entered the place where he was working. "I didn't see Him, but I knew He was there," he said. He had been sinking down in despair, but this experience lifted him up for a time. I was never able to get him to talk about the Bible in any coherent, sensible way. He had little interest in God's word, or in prayer, or in serving Christ. This one experience was his basis for assurance that all was well between him and the Lord.

Unless people are well grounded in Scripture, they are apt to trust in their unusual experiences, not realizing that such things are unreliable. Jonathan Edwards, who carefully studied people affected by the Great Awakening in America during the 1740s, concluded that visions, voices, and other vivid experiences were not directly from God (as some assumed) or from the devil (as opponents of the revival insisted). They were, in modern terminology, psychologically induced, and they were therefore of no value in determining a person's spiritual state. His Scottish contemporaries kept careful records of people who made professions of faith during that time. Nine years after the outbreak of revival, several churches evaluated the spiritual standing of the people who had apparently been converted during the awakening. The evaluation of elders of the church at Cambuslang is typical.

> *Though the most of the subjects of the awakening, whose exercise contained a mixture of strong fancy and imagination, are relapsed to their former sinful courses: yet, there are several instances of persons, whose exercises were mixed with fanciful apprehensions; and which they gave out to be real representations of objects and visions, [who] are of the number of those who are persevering in a justifiable Christian profession, and unblemished conversation.*[2]

---

[2] James Robe, *Narratives of the Extraordinary Work of the Spirit of God, at Cambuslang, Kilsyth, &c. Begun 1742* (Glasgow: David Niven, 1790), 319.

In other words, most people who had visions or heard voices at that time fell back into the mud holes of sin (2 Peter 2:20-22), but a few continued to give a credible profession of faith. Trusting in some apparently supernatural experience is not the same as trusting in Christ. People who trust in religious experiences are in no better shape than those who trust in their own excellence. It is only trust in Christ that saves.

Instead of trusting in of Christ, lame ducks may trust in their own emotions. In the parable of the sower, Jesus described how various kinds of soils received the word of God.

> *The one on whom seed was sown on the rocky places, this is the man who hears the word and immediately receives it with joy; yet he has no firm root in himself, but is only temporary, and when affliction or persecution arises because of the word, immediately he falls away (Matthew 13:20-21).*

Great joy often accompanies genuine faith and salvation, but people who falsely think they are saved can also feel great joy. They pray the sinner's prayer; someone tells them their sins are forgiven; and they are happy. Praying a prayer is not necessarily the same as repentance and faith, but a superficial believer's sense of relief often causes him to conclude that his faith is genuine.

Many such people eventually turn away from Christ altogether.

Another emotion that may be a counterfeit for true faith is sorrow over sin. There is such a thing as godly sorrow, but not all sorrow is of that nature.

> *I now rejoice, not that you were made sorrowful, but that you were made sorrowful to the point of repentance; for you were made sorrowful according to the will of God, so that you might not suffer loss in anything through us. For the sorrow that is according to the will of God produces a repentance without regret, leading to salvation, but the sorrow of the world produces death" (2 Corinthians 7:9-10).*

Judas Iscariot provides striking example of the sorrow that does not lead to repentance. After betraying Christ, he was suddenly overwhelmed with guilt and remorse. This was not a saving sorrow, for Jesus called him "the son of perdition" (John 17:12). The sorrow of Judas was the sorrow of the world that leads to death, and it led him to commit suicide by hanging himself (Matthew 27:1-5). There is a great difference between a sensitive conscience that leads God's children to avoid sin and a guilty sorrow that produces despair and hopelessness without repentance and change.

I remember one man telling me that he wasn't really so bad because he still felt sorry for his sins. That did not, apparently, mean he was going to make any changes or even that he was going to humble himself before the Lord. I have deep concerns about his relationship to Jesus Christ.

Lame ducks may believe they have genuine faith because of joy or sorrow that imitates the joy or sorrow of God's children. If so, they are trusting in their emotions rather than in Christ.

Limping Christians differ from lame ducks in their perseverance through trials.

The book of Hebrews was written to Jews who had professed faith in Christ. They had been baptized and had joined the church. Now they were being challenged by Jews who were trying to draw them away from Christ. Persecution was mounting, and the lure of the old sacrificial system was very strong, so they were in danger of casting aside their confidence in Christ and going back to Judaism. Several passages in Hebrews issue stern warnings about deserting Christ. Chapter 10 encourages the believers not to forsake the Christian assembly. Then the author issues one of the strongest threats in the Bible.

> *For if we go on sinning willfully after receiving the knowledge of the truth, there no longer remains a sacrifice for sins, but a terrifying expectation of judgment and the fury of a fire which will consume the adversaries. Anyone who has set aside the Law of Moses dies without mercy on the testimony of two or three witnesses. How much severer punishment do you think he will deserve who has trampled under foot the Son of God, and has regarded as unclean the blood of the covenant by which he was sanctified, and has insulted the Spirit of grace? For we know Him who said, "Vengeance is mine, I will repay." And again, "The Lord will judge His people." It is a terrifying thing to fall into the hands of the living God (Hebrews 10:26-31).*

This passage used to frighten me. I knew that my sin was not accidental. I knew that I made deliberate, sinful choices. My will was corrupt. Later on, I realized that "sinning willfully" is not just any sin. It is the sin of casting Christ aside and turning against Him. It is the sin of apostasy.

When lame ducks become disillusioned, they desert Christ. When they first make a profession of faith in Christ, they think that God will make their way smooth, so when their life becomes difficult, they bail out. They say, "I prayed, and God didn't give me a good job. I was a good person, and God didn't take care of me. This Christianity business is not working."

Perhaps, instead of a personal disappointment, they look at the horrible suffering that people around the world endure. Then they hear that God is sovereign. He is in control of everything that happens. They do not understand the link between sin and suffering. They do not see the Bible's big picture and what God's plan for this world really is.[3] They say, "If I were God, I could sure do a better job of running the world than He does. I'm not going to believe in Him anymore."

The reasons for disillusionment are many: a broken marriage, the death of a child, a financial collapse, a pastor who betrayed his calling by running off with the church secretary. The disillusioned deserter says, "God failed. I quit."

When limping Christians are tested by difficulties, they persevere. They may stum-

---

[3] For a discussion of God's reasons for permitting sin and suffering to enter His world, see my book, *The Beauty of God for a Broken World: Reflections on the Goodness of the God of the Bible* (Fort Washington, PA: CLCPublications, 2010), chapters 1, 8, 9, and Appendix 3.

ble, and fall, but they don't stay down. "For a righteous man falls seven times, and rises again, But the wicked stumble in time of calamity" (Proverbs 24:16).

One of the great differences between a limping Christian and a lame duck is that the limping Christian keeps hobbling along. In *Pilgrim's Progress, the Second Part,* Mr. Feeble-mind says,

> *I have resolved on, to wit, to run when I can, to go when I cannot run, and to creep when I cannot go. As to the main, I thank Him that loves me, I am fixed. My way is before me, my mind is beyond the river that has no bridge, though I am, as you see, but of a feeble mind.[4]*

The lame duck, who turns away from Christ, is captured and wolfed down by the devil, but the faith of the limping Christian remains. After warning us about the danger of apostasy, the author of Hebrews encourages us to persevere.

> *Therefore, do not throw away your confidence, which has a great reward. For you have need of endurance, so that when you have done the will of God, you may receive what was promised. For yet in a very little while, he who is coming will come, and will not delay. But My righteous one shall live*

---

[4] Bunyan, 78-79.

by faith; and if he shrinks back, My soul has no pleasure in him. But we are not of those who shrink back to destruction, but of those who have faith to the preserving of the soul (Hebrews 10:35-39).

Limping progress is still progress. The man or woman who limps toward heaven will eventually arrive even though his journey is harder than it needs to be.

Do you think you may not be saved? Well, then, do you dare to cast Christ aside and trample on His blood? "NO! NO!" you say. "I would never do that. I love Him too much. I want Him. I need Him. He is my only hope." Then do not be afraid. If you will not part with Christ, He will not part with you.

In an old story, a tortoise and a hare engage in a foot race. The hare quickly outpaces the tortoise. After he has gained a considerable lead, the hare lies down for a nap, while the plodding tortoise passes him and wins the race. Even a tortoise with a broken leg may eventually cross the finish line. So can you, even if you are limping all the way.

Not to the strong is the battle,
Not to the swift is the race,
Yet to the true and the faithful
Vict'ry is promised through grace.[5]

You fearful trembling ones who cling to Christ—you will finish the race because Jesus will hold you up. You may limp and even fall down, but by His grace you will not stay down. God has promised victory to everyone who clings trustingly to Christ.

For whatever is born of God overcomes the world; and this is the victory that has overcome the world—our faith. Who is the one who overcomes the world, but he who believes that Jesus is the Son of God (1 John 5:4-5)?

---

[5] This is the chorus of "Victory through Grace" written by Fanny Crosby under the pseudonym Sally Martin.

CHAPTER 3
IBUPROFEN FOR
LIMPING CHRISTIANS

It was interesting to watch my wife's gradual recovery from her knee replacement. One thing we noticed during the first two weeks is that when she didn't take her pain medications, she could not do her exercises. The pain pills did not do anything to promote healing directly, but they made it possible for her to do what she needed to do in order to become stronger and regain her range of motion. At first, she was on prescription painkillers, but then she switched to ibuprofen.

You may never have had a knee replaced, but perhaps you have sprained an ankle, broken a wrist, or torn a rotator cuff. You know that aspirin or ibuprofen, cannot cure those problems, but it may provide temporary relief so that you are able keep moving.

In this chapter, I will not say much about healing for your spiritual limp (though I will come to that later). All I want to do is to give your painful joints some relief so that you can keep on going. It is possible that you will limp all the way from here to heaven. After God wrestled all night with Jacob, He touched the socket of Jacob's thigh so that he limped the rest of his life. God used that limp to humble him and give him spiritual victory. (Genesis 32:24-32; Hosea 12:2-5).

Even if your limp is not completely healed in this life, the Bible offers you spiritual ibuprofen to relieve the pain when you fall and to give you enough mobility to get up again. This chapter contains three tablets of spiritual ibuprofen. Feel free to take them as needed.

The first ibuprofen tablet is for terrible trials.

Job is a book about suffering. It asks the question, *Why do good people suffer?* The answer comes in two parts. First, good people do not suffer because they are secret sinners. Second, God is good and just, mighty and majestic, and He is not going to tell you why you are suffering, so kwitcherbellyachin.

The first two chapters, tell us that God allowed Satan to kill Job's ten children, take away his wealth in livestock, and smite him "with sore boils from the sole of his foot to the crown of his head" (2:7). Then Job went out, sat on the ash heap as a sign of mourning, and scraped his puss-filled boils with a piece of broken pottery. In spite of his suffering, Job did not abandon his faith in God.

> *But it is still my consolation,*
> *And I rejoice in unsparing pain,*
> *That I have not denied the words of the Holy*
>   *One (Job 6:10).*
> *Though He slay me, I will hope in Him (Job*
>   *13:15).*
> *But He knows the way I take;*
> *When He has tried me, I shall come forth as*
>   *gold (Job 23:10).*

James 5:11 commends Job for his endurance in the midst of trials, but he sure did a wheelbarrow load of complaining.

Job complained about God's dealings with him. He began by cursing the day of his birth.

> *Let the day perish on which I was to be born,*
> *And the night which said, "A boy is*
>   *conceived."*
> *May that day be darkness;*
> *Let not God above care for it,*
> *Nor light shine on it.*
> *Let darkness and black gloom claim it;*
> *Let a cloud settle on it;*
> *Let the blackness of the day terrify it.*
> *As for that night, let darkness seize it;*
> *Let it not rejoice among the days of the year;*
> *Let it not come into the number of the months.*
> *Behold, let that night be barren;*
> *Let no joyful shout enter it.*
> *Let those curse it who curse the day,*
> *Who are prepared to rouse Leviathan.*

Let the stars of its twilight be darkened;
Let it wait for light but have none,
And let it not see the breaking dawn;
Because it did not shut the opening of my
*   mother's womb,*
Or hide trouble from my eyes.
Why did I not die at birth,
Come forth from the womb and expire?
Why did the knees receive me,
And why the breasts, that I should suck?
For now I would have lain down and been
*   quiet;*
I would have slept then, I would have been at
*   rest,*
With kings and with counselors of the earth,
Who rebuilt ruins for themselves;
Or with princes who had gold,
Who were filling their houses with silver.
Or like a miscarriage which is discarded, I
*   would not be,*
As infants that never saw light.
There the wicked cease from raging,
And there the weary are at rest.
The prisoners are at ease together;
They do not hear the voice of the taskmaster.
The small and the great are there,
And the slave is free from his master.
Why is light given to him who suffers,
And life to the bitter of soul,
Who long for death, but there is none,
And dig for it more than for hidden treasures,
Who rejoice greatly,
And exult when they find the grave?
Why is light given to a man whose way is
*   hidden,*

And whom God has hedged in?
For my groaning comes at the sight of my
*   food,*
And my cries pour out like water.
For what I fear comes upon me,
And what I dread befalls me.
I am not at ease, nor am I quiet,
And I am not at rest, but turmoil comes (Job
*   3:3-26).*

I have heard many people complain and a few wish that they were dead, but they are all rank amateurs compared to Job. Most people just whine the same tune over and over. Job is history's most expressive mourner. He is by turns angry, frustrated, and belligerent, but he is always eloquent. As the book unfolds, he argues with his finger-pointing friends; he protests his innocence, and he comes very close to accusing God of being unjust. He keeps demanding that God answer him. Finally, God does.

God confronted Job with His majesty and power.

Then the Lord answered Job out of the whirlwind and said, "Who is this that darkens counsel by words without knowledge? Now gird up your loins like a man, and I will ask you, and you instruct Me" (Job 38:1-3)!

The Lord spent the next two chapters asking Job a series of questions he could not answer. He challenged Job to match His power and wisdom as revealed in the created world. Then He said to Job, "Will the faultfinder contend with the Almighty? Let him who reproves God answer it." Job responded with appropriate humility, "Behold, I am insignificant; what can I reply to You? I lay my hand on my mouth" (Job 40:1-4). Nevertheless, the Lord was not done with him. God's assault on Job's ignorance and weakness continued for two more chapters. Finally, the ordeal was over.

> *Then Job answered the Lord and said,*
> *"I know that You can do all things,*
> *And that no purpose of Yours can be*
>   *thwarted....*
> *Therefore I have declared that which I did not*
>   *understand,*
> *Things too wonderful for me, which I did not*
>   *know....*
> *I have heard of You by the hearing of the ear;*
> *But now my eye sees You;*
> *Therefore I retract,*
> *And I repent in dust and ashes" (Job 42:1-6).*

When God confronted Job, He did not tell Job why he was suffering. He basically said, "I'm God. You're not. That's all you need to know." At this point in the book, we are ready to write Job off as a futile complainer, a loser, a reject, a failure. God put him to the test, and he flunked. We are not prepared for God's last word.

God commended Job. Throughout the book, Job's friends insisted that Job was a terrible (though secret) sinner. Otherwise, God would not have punished him so harshly. Job knew that he was not sinless, but he kept insisting that he was innocent of their charges. He refused to deny the Lord, and he steadfastly maintained confidence in his final vindication: "But He knows the way I take; when He has tried me, I shall come forth as gold" (23:10). In the end, God agreed with Job rather than with his friends.

> *It came about after the Lord had spoken these words to Job, that the Lord said to Eliphaz the Temanite, "My wrath is kindled against you and against your two friends, because you have not spoken of Me what is right as My servant Job has. Now therefore, take for yourselves seven bulls and seven rams, and go to My servant Job, and offer up a burnt offering for yourselves, and My servant Job will pray for you. For I will accept him so that I may not do with you according to your folly, because you have not spoken of Me what is right, as My servant Job has." So Eliphaz the Temanite and Bildad the Shuhite and Zophar the Naamathite went and did as the Lord told them; and the Lord accepted Job (Job 42:7-9).*

On top of that, God gave Job ten more children and twice as much wealth as he had at the beginning of the book.

In spite of all Job's complaining, in spite of all Job's challenges and questions, God loved and accepted Job. I find that extremely encouraging. Child of God, when you are overwhelmed by one catastrophe after another, when you cry out to God for answers and He is silent, when your soul is as loathsome in your sight as Job's oozing boils were in his, God loves you and accepts you because you belong to Jesus.

The life of Job is a spiritual ibuprofen tablet to ease your pain when you are enduring terrible trials. The book's raw emotions and even the harsh tone of God's confrontation with Job give comfort and courage to keep you limping hopefully on your way to glory.

The second ibuprofen tablet is for fearsome falls.

For this tablet, we are going to look at the life of the apostle Peter. The point I want to make is that Jesus will pick you up as He did Peter. On the night before His crucifixion, Jesus predicted that all of the apostles would desert Him. Peter proudly boasted that even if all the rest ran away, he would not. His pride would have led to a deadly fall except for one thing.

Jesus requested help for Peter. Before Jesus told Peter that he would deny his Lord, Jesus reassured Peter that his fall would not be fatal.

> "Simon, Simon, behold, Satan has demanded permission to sift you like wheat; but I have prayed for you, that your faith may not fail; and you, when once you have turned again, strengthen your brothers." But he said to Him, "Lord, with You I am ready to go both to prison and to death!" And He said, "I say to you, Peter, the rooster will not crow today until you have denied three times that you know Me" (Luke 22:31-34).

Peter did deny the Lord that night. His courage failed, but not his faith because it was impossible that the Father would not answer the prayer of His beloved Son. If you belong to Christ, He is praying now for you. Your courage may fail. Your strength may give out. You may experience a grievous fall, but because of the prayers of Jesus, your faith will not fail. As your high priest, He continually pleads your case before the Father (Romans 8:34; Hebrews 2:17; 4:14-16). "Therefore He is able to save forever those who draw near to God through Him, since He always lives

to make intercession for them" (Hebrews 7:25).
Our Lord, however, did more than pray for His
apostle.

Jesus reached out to Peter. After He rose
from the grave, and before He appeared to the
gathered apostles, He held three private inter-
views. First, Jesus met Mary Magdalene. We
know what they said to each other. Second, He
walked with two unnamed disciples who had left
Jerusalem for their home in Emmaus. We know
the gist of their conversation. The third was His
appearance to Peter. We know nothing at all
about that conversation (Luke 24:34; 1 Corinthians 15:5).

Jesus appeared to Peter. That is all we know,
but that is enough. Jesus reached out and down
to the genuine apostle who had fallen the fur-
thest, and He restored Peter to His favor. The
Lord rebuked Peter with a look after Peter's third
denial (Luke 22:61), but He did not reject him.
Instead, when He came out of the grave, He
found this broken man and lifted him up.

Jesus will not kick you when you are down,
either. Perhaps you have sinned grievously. Perhaps you think there is no road that will take you
back into the Savior's favor. You cannot climb
back up to God, which is why He has come down
to you. When you are at your lowest, look for His

outstretched hand. Lift up your feeble hand to Him, and you will find that He is already reaching down to you.

Even when God's erring children finally become convinced that they are forgiven and accepted, they often assume that their days of useful service are over. Happily, Peter's story demonstrates that this is not the case.

Jesus recommissioned Peter. Sometime later, the risen Jesus met Peter and several other apostles after a night of fruitless fishing. The Lord not only gave them a great catch of fish; He also fixed breakfast for them.

> *So when they had finished breakfast, Jesus said to Simon Peter, "Simon, son of John, do you love Me more than these?" He said to Him, "Yes, Lord; You know that I love You." He said to him, "Tend My lambs." He said to him again a second time, "Simon, son of John, do you love Me?" He said to Him, "Yes, Lord; You know that I love You." He said to him, "Shepherd My sheep." He said to him the third time, "Simon, son of John, do you love Me?" Peter was grieved because He said to him the third time, "Do you love Me?" And he said to Him, "Lord, You know all things; You know that I love You." Jesus said to him, "Tend My sheep" (John 21:15-17).*

Do you love Me more than these? Before Jesus was crucified, Peter had boldly announced that even if the rest of the apostles deserted Christ, he would stand firm. Now when Jesus asks whether Peter loves Him more than the other disciples do, Peter will not make such a boast. His reply means, *I love You, I have great and warm affection for you, but I will not compare myself to the others.*

Peter was grieved that Jesus questioned his love three times because it reminded him of his three denials. It might have felt as if Jesus doubted his love. That was not the case because after each question, Jesus reaffirmed Peter's role as a shepherd of Christ's sheep.

This is a wonderfully encouraging passage. When you have fallen into sin or failed the Lord very badly, you may wonder whether the Lord will ever use you again. See how gracious He is! Jesus not only forgave Peter, He set him on the path of future service. Sometimes, it is true, our sin mars our usefulness, but Jesus will always find some use for a repentant disciple. He will find some use for you. Peter's experience is a spiritual ibuprofen tablet to ease your grief and to give you courage to get up when you have stumbled and fallen.

The third ibuprofen tablet is for feeble faith.

In the gospel of Matthew, Jesus frequently chides His disciples for their little faith. Taken together these examples provide relief for distress when your faith is small.

Be encouraged when your faith seems too little to trust in God's provision. It is natural for us to worry when we cannot figure out how to pay the bills. It is even worse for those who are shivering in the cold or those who do not know where their next meal is coming from. Jesus reminds us that God feeds the birds, and He clothes the wild flowers with beautiful blooms. Then He adds,

> But if God so clothes the grass of the field, which is alive today and tomorrow is thrown into the furnace, will He not much more clothe you? You of little faith! Do not worry then, saying, "What will we eat?" or "What will we drink?" or "What will we wear for clothing?" For the Gentiles eagerly seek all these things; for your heavenly Father knows that you need all these things. But seek first His kingdom and His righteousness, and all these things will be added to you. So do not worry about tomorrow; for tomorrow will care for itself. Each day has enough trouble of its own (Matthew 6:30-34).

I find it encouraging that the Lord did **not** say, "If your faith is little, God will let you starve." Instead, He tells us that even though we may be people of little faith, God will take care of us. Therefore, do not fret. Do not worry.

The disciples had a hard time learning this lesson.

> *And the disciples came to the other side of the sea, but they had forgotten to bring any bread. And Jesus said to them, "Watch out and beware of the leaven of the Pharisees and Sadducees." They began to discuss this among themselves, saying, "He said that because we did not bring any bread." But Jesus, aware of this, said, "You men of little faith, why do you discuss among yourselves that you have no bread? Do you not yet understand or remember the five loaves of the five thousand, and how many baskets full you picked up? Or the seven loaves of the four thousand, and how many large baskets full you picked up? How is it that you do not understand that I did not speak to you concerning bread? But beware of the leaven of the Pharisees and Sadducees." Then they understood that He did not say to beware of the leaven of bread, but of the teaching of the Pharisees and Sadducees (Matthew 16:5-12).*

Matthew 14 reports the feeding of the 5,000. Matthew 15 reports the feeding of the 4,000.[6] Matthew 16 shows us that the disciples still had very small faith when it came to trusting in God's provision for their needs. The encouraging thing is that Jesus did not throw up His hands in disgust and say, "Go away you unbelievers. Feed yourselves. I'm not going to bother to take care of you anymore." Even though their faith was little, it was still faith. Jesus did not kick them off His team and choose a whole new batch of apostles.

Be encouraged when your faith seems too little to rest in God's protection. Matthew tells us about two difficult passages across the stormy Sea of Galilee.

When He got into the boat, His disciples followed Him. And behold, there arose a great storm on the sea, so that the boat was being covered with the waves; but Jesus Himself was asleep. And they came to Him

---

[6] These chapters and numbers are easy to remember if you note the numbers in bold type that add up to nine. (This, by the way, has no spiritual significance. It is just a bit of interesting trivia. However, if I were a medieval allegorist, I might note that 9 = 3 x 3; since there are 3 persons in the Trinity, I might then see the feeding of the 9,000 as symbolic of the Trinity.)
Matthew 14 5,000 fed and 4 + 5 = 9
Matthew 15 4,000 fed and 5 + 4 = 9
         29 9,000 fed

and woke Him, saying, "Save us, Lord; we are perishing!" He said to them, "Why are you afraid, you men of little faith?" Then He got up and rebuked the winds and the sea, and it became perfectly calm. The men were amazed, and said, "What kind of a man is this, that even the winds and the sea obey Him" (Matthew 8:23-27)?

The disciples doubted God's protection, but Jesus took care of them anyway. That is a great comfort. After the feeding of the 5,000, we have another example of little faith that is nevertheless genuine faith. Jesus sent the twelve away in a boat while He dismissed the crowds and then went up on a mountain to pray.

But the boat was already a long distance from the land, battered by the waves; for the wind was contrary. And in the fourth watch of the night He came to them, walking on the sea. When the disciples saw Him walking on the sea, they were terrified, and said, "It is a ghost!" And they cried out in fear. But immediately Jesus spoke to them, saying, "Take courage, it is I; do not be afraid." Peter said to Him, "Lord, if it is You, command me to come to You on the water." And He said, "Come!" And Peter got out of the boat, and walked on the water and came toward Jesus. But seeing the wind, he became frightened, and beginning to sink, he cried out, "Lord, save me!" Immediately Jesus stretched out His hand and took hold of him, and said to him, "You of little faith, why did you doubt?" When they got into the boat, the wind stopped. And those who were in the boat worshiped Him, saying, "You are certainly God's Son!" (Matthew 14:24-33).

Jesus did not reprimand them for their initial fear. He only reproached Peter for his small faith. Peter had some faith because he did get out of the boat and walk on the water toward Jesus. (To me that seems like great faith!) Nevertheless, when Peter's faith faltered, Jesus did not let him drown.

When you are looking at the angry waves of temptations, trials, and the terrors of the devil, it is not the greatness of your faith that protects you. Jesus protects you. Take comfort in His loving care, not in the magnitude of your faith.

Be encouraged when your faith seems too little to draw on God's power. When Jesus chose His twelve apostles, He "gave them authority over unclean spirits, to cast them out, and to heal every kind of disease and every kind of sickness" (Matthew 10:1). It must have been thrilling for these men to touch lepers and heal them and to speak to demons and have them flee, but on one occasion, they failed utterly. Jesus came down from the mount of transfiguration to find a crowd surrounding His flummoxed followers.

> *When they came to the crowd, a man came up to Jesus, falling on his knees before Him and saying, "Lord, have mercy on my son, for he is a lunatic and is very ill; for he often falls into the fire and often into the water. I brought him to Your disciples, and they could not cure him." And Jesus answered and said, "You unbelieving and perverted generation, how long shall I be with you? How long shall I put up with you? Bring him here to Me." And Jesus rebuked him, and the demon came out of him, and the boy was cured at once. Then the disciples came to Jesus privately and said, "Why could we not drive it out?" And He said to them, "Because of the littleness of your faith; for truly I say to you, if you have faith the size of a mustard seed, you will say to this mountain, 'Move from here to there,' and it will move; and nothing will be impossible to you" (Matthew 17:14-20).*

The apostles were frustrated and puzzled by their failure. What was wrong? Why were they unable to cast out the demon? The problem was with their faith. Their faith must have been smaller than a mustard seed, and their prayers were correspondingly weak.

Again, this is an encouragement to us when our faith is weak and even smaller than a mustard seed. We ask for great miracles, and we do not see them. Our faith is little, and we feel worthless. Do not let that stop you. Jesus healed the boy after their faith faltered. He did what they were unable to do. That is always true. The completion of God's plans and the fulfillment of His purposes depend on His own mighty power, not on the size of our faith. The work of God shall be done, and we will have an opportunity to be amazed and to praise His holy name.

This is a very useful doctrine for us.

Though God tries and tests us, He will never crush us. Jesus will not break the bruised reed or extinguish the smoking wick (Isaiah 42:3; Matthew 12:20).

The Lord did not reject these limping believers. He did not reject Job in spite of all his complaining. He did not reject Peter in spite of his denying Jesus three times. He did not reject the apostles in spite of the littleness of their faith. If, like a baby bird, you have come under the shelter of His wings, He will keep you safe. He will not allow the giant Despair to crush the life out of you; He will not allow the flaming trials to burn you or the waters of guilt and hopelessness to drown your faith (Isaiah 43:2).

The Lord did mildly rebuke these limping believers. God spoke to Job out of the whirlwind. He took four strong chapters to put Job in his place. The rebuke of God stung, no doubt about that. Job repented in dust and ashes (42:6), but God did not burn him to a crisp or turn him into dust and ashes.

Jesus' rebuke of Peter was even gentler. He did not stop with asking, *"Do you love me"* three times. That would have been a painful reproach. After Peter confessed his love, the Lord reinstated him as a shepherd of His sheep.

Jesus repeatedly chided His apostles for their little faith, but He accepted their little faith as genuine faith. Then He accomplished His will by His own power in spite of their faltering faith.

In the same way, the Spirit of Christ will rebuke you and me for our complaining attitude, our sinful falls, and our little faith. He is not pleased with these things in our lives, and He will not be silent about them, but the Lord's rebukes are far milder than we deserve. He treats us as a father does his children, not as a judge treats a repeat offender. God does not lynch His children. He does not toss them in the slammer and throw away the key. He gently rebukes us because He wants us to repent, and He wants us to repent in order that He may hold us close in a loving hug.

The Lord gently restored these limping believers. I said at the beginning of this chapter that you might limp all the way to heaven. After Jacob wrestled with the angel of the Lord, he limped for the rest of his life (Genesis 32:31). Paul carried a thorn in his flesh all of his days (2 Corinthians 12:7-10). However, Jacob's limp and Paul's thorn had the same spiritual purpose—to humble them and to increase their dependence on the strength of God. Though Jacob and Paul continued to limp in one way, God made them stronger in other ways.

Job, Peter and the rest of the apostles came through their dark times of despair and doubting into the bright light of God's blessing. That is what God wants to do for you as well. He may leave you limping in some respects, but only to make you more dependent on His strength. He wants you to do well. He wants to restore to you the joy of your salvation. He wants to increase your usefulness and to give you greater joy in Christ than you have ever known.

A Parable: Mary Jones

We sinners must not fall into the trap of thinking that God is only pleased with perfection. If we do, we may either persuade ourselves that we are better than we are, or we may become so discouraged that we give up the battle. God is glorified as you and I struggle against sin. Every victory, no matter how small, brings glory to Him because it is the work of the Holy Spirit within us.

Come with me to the heavenly Jerusalem, which is both our mother and our proper home. As we approach the holy city, we see two angels standing beside a gate carved from one immense pearl. Their faces shine like the noonday sun, reflecting the glory of God. Notice how intently the angels are watching something on earth below. From a small town in Nebraska a light has broken forth, a light that is far brighter and more glorious than the glowing faces of the angels. What can it be?

The angels are watching Mary Jones. There must be thousands of young ladies named Mary Jones, some of them rich, some beautiful, some intelligent. Our Mary Jones is none of these. No one except her mother has ever said she was pretty. She isn't homely either, just very ordinary. She is also very special because she is a Christian and because right now she is winning an important spiritual battle. Let's see what it is.

Mary Jones had a boyfriend once. They even talked about marriage, but during her senior year of high school her father died, and her mother came down with cancer. Mary was the only child, and there was no one else to help at home. Her young man became tired of trips to the hospital and long waits at doctors' offices, so gradually he drifted away. Mary's mother lingered on for three years, but when she finally passed away, Mary entered a two-year secretarial program at the local junior college. At first she worked nights as a waitress, but in her last term she landed a sec-retarial position in the afternoons. It was just the kind of job she had always wanted, and it was to become full-time when she graduated.

Mary was very lonely. Most of the young men she had known in high school were married or had moved away. That is reason she responded so warmly to the kindness of the office manager, Mr. Wilson. Sometimes they took lunch together. Mr. Wilson was married, but Mary thought eve-rything was all right because they were "just friends." Everything was all right, that is, until

Mr. Wilson invited her to spend the weekend with him while his wife was visiting her parents.

Mary endured a terrible struggle. She felt very close to Mr. Wilson. She even dreamed about him at times, and she wanted to be with him, but something held her back. That something was the honor of Jesus Christ. How could she bring shame on His precious name by committing adultery?

At first, she told Mr. Wilson she would think about his proposition. Then she made up some excuse about a prior commitment, but she felt like a traitor to Christ because she could not bring herself to speak openly of her Lord to her boss. When the second invitation came, the accusations of her heart became almost intolerable. At the same time, her fantasies about Mr. Wilson began to increase, and she could feel herself weakening. In desperation, she ran to an older Christian lady who listened to her, prayed with her, and agreed to ask her once a week whether her chastity was still intact.

Three days later Mary scheduled a private conference at the office with Mr. Wilson. She told him that she was a Christian, that adultery was a sin and that she wanted to protect the honor of Jesus' name. "Furthermore," she said, "if I sleep with you, I will have to tell my friend, and she will tell my pastor, and my pastor will call you. Those are the arrangements I have made."

Mr. Wilson was furious. Tension at the office mounted, and a week later, he fired her and sent a negative evaluation back to her college. Mary was devastated. She was too ashamed of her own attraction to Mr. Wilson to say anything at school about his behavior, so the college placement office accepted his report at face value. Her grades began to drop; another comparable position seemed like a hopeless dream, and she was almost broke. In her own eyes, she was a failure.

BUT up in heaven the angels are watching Mary, and they see a bright and glorious light. They marvel that a little town in Nebraska could house such splendor. Mary Jones does not know anything about that, but she has brought great glory to God.

Perhaps I have the town wrong. It may be Jackson, Mississippi, or Newark, New Jersey, or even Allentown, Pennsylvania. Perhaps the name is wrong, and the temptation as well. Perhaps it is really you the angels are watching. They behold your struggles, your discouragement, your hesitation, and they marvel over your victory, as your desire to honor the name of Christ finally brings you through into the light of God's glory.

CHAPTER 4
THE PHYSICIAN FOR
LIMPING CHRISTIANS

In 1990 President George H. W. Bush signed the Americans with Disabilities Act. Because of that Act, we have become accustomed to seeing sidewalks with cutouts for wheel chairs, handicapped-accessible bathrooms, and signs in Braille. (I fail understand the need for those. If a person could see to find the sign in the first place, it would not need to be in Braille.)

Heather and I have been to Russia and Turkey several times and to Senegal once. We can assure you that those countries do not have any requirements to accommodate the handicapped. (I would like to know how a physically disabled person uses a squatty potty.) I suspect that many other countries are not very friendly to the handicapped.

I know some jokes about handicapped people, and I am sinful enough to have shared them and laughed at them. God, on the other hand, reserves His laughter for rebellious sinners (Psalm 2:4). He never laughs at the handicapped. "You shall not curse a deaf man, nor place a stumbling block before the blind, but you shall revere your God; I am the LORD" (Leviticus 19:14). When Job was protesting his innocence to his three accusing friends, one of the things he said was, "I was eyes to the blind and feet to the lame" (Job 29:15). God cares deeply for the handicapped.

Throughout the Bible, physical afflictions are frequently symbols for national or individual sins and sorrows. Physical and spiritual lameness blend together in some Old Testament prophecies of Messiah's reign and in our Lord's healing ministry.

> *Say to those with anxious heart,*
> *"Take courage, fear not.*
> *Behold, your God will come with vengeance;*
> *The recompense of God will come,*
> *But He will save you."*
> *Then the eyes of the blind will be opened*
> *And the ears of the deaf will be unstopped.*
> *Then the lame will leap like a deer,*
> *And the tongue of the mute will shout for joy.*
> *For waters will break forth in the wilderness*
> *And streams in the Arabah [the desert]*
>   *(Isaiah 35:4-6).*

This prophecy received its initial fulfillment at the first coming of Jesus. When John the Baptist sent disciples to ask Jesus if He was the one promised by God, He answered them first with deeds, then with words.

At that very time He cured many people of diseases and afflictions and evil spirits; and He gave sight to many who were blind. And He answered and said to them, "Go and report to John what you have seen and heard: the blind receive sight, the lame walk, the lepers are cleansed, and the deaf hear, the dead are raised up, the poor have the gospel preached to them. Blessed is he who does not take offense at Me" (Luke 7:21-23).

Jesus healed many lame people, and in the name of Jesus, the apostles Peter and Paul healed men born lame. In both cases, the lame men *leaped up* (Acts 3:8; 14:10), just as Isaiah had said they would do: "the lame will *leap* like a deer."

Limping Christians have a lame leg (or maybe two). Their gait is uneven. They stumble often because of certain hindrances and sins that trip them up. Probably most of us feel like limping Christians at one time or another. The good news is that Jesus still heals lame believers.

Jesus heals by His powerful word

God is a speaking God. In the Bible, we do not see God doing random miracles without telling His people anything about them. He speaks a word of command, and what He says comes to pass. In Genesis 1, each act of creation is preceded by the phrase, "Then God said." Psalm 33 summarizes God's work of creation in a single sentence: "By the word of the LORD the heavens were made, and by the breath of His mouth all their host" (v. 6). Likewise, when God brought Israel out of Egypt, He spoke through Moses before He sent each of the ten plagues.

How are people saved? Only through faith in Christ. Where does that faith come from? "So faith comes from hearing, and hearing by the word of Christ" (Romans 10:17). God always works in our lives through His word.

Jesus spoke to heal physical afflictions. After He rebuked a demon and cast it out of a man,

> ... amazement came upon them all, and they began talking with one another saying, "What is this message [literally, "word"]? For with authority and power He commands the unclean spirits and they come out." And the report about Him was spreading into every locality in the surrounding district. Then He got up and left the synagogue, and entered Simon's home. Now Simon's mother-in-law was suffering from a high fever, and they asked Him to help her. And standing over her, He rebuked the fever, and it left her; and she immediately got up and waited on them (Luke 4:36-39).

Jesus did not do some magical manipulations or speak a mysterious spell in order to send demons packing. People were used to the Jewish exorcists going through all sorts of mumbo jumbo when they pretended to cast out evil spirits. The thing that impressed the people about Jesus was the power of His word. He spoke, and the demons had to obey. The fever of Peter's mother-in-law was, no doubt, caused by a bacterium, a virus, or a parasite, but when Jesus spoke, the fever went away. The word of Jesus had power over demons, disease, and even death.

To a little girl who had died, He said "'Talitha kum!' (which translated means, 'Little girl, I say to you, get up!')," and she did (Mark 5:41). At the open tomb of Lazarus, He cried out, "Lazarus, come forth," and the corpse obeyed (John 11:43).

Jesus heals by His powerful word. That is what He did when He walked the land of Palestine two millennia ago. That is still how He works in our lives today.

The Lord heals spiritual ills through His written word. The psalmist exclaimed, "If Your law had not been my delight, then I would have perished in my affliction. I will never forget Your precepts, for by them You have revived me" (Psalm 119:92-93). When we are in a low, depressed condition, God's word is the instrument by which He renews our spirits and lifts us up to joy.

> *Let the word of Christ richly dwell within you, with all wisdom teaching and admonishing one another with psalms and hymns and spiritual songs, singing with thankfulness in your hearts to God (Colossians 3:15-16).*

The "word of Christ" means either the word about Christ (the gospel) or the word from Christ (the message that the Lord gave through His prophets and apostles). In either case, we get the word of Christ only from the Bible. If you want to have a happy, singing, thankful heart, the word of Christ must dwell richly within you—not haphazardly, not occasionally, not in small doses, but richly.

When our lives are barren and fruitless, the answer again comes through the word of our Lord.

> *I am the true vine, and My Father is the vinedresser. Every branch in Me that does not bear fruit, He takes away; and every branch that bears fruit, He prunes [or cleans] it so that it may bear more fruit. You are already clean [or pruned] because of the word which I have spoken to you (John 15:1-3).*

Holiness is another result of the Bible's work in our lives. The night before His crucifixion, Jesus prayed for all of His disciples throughout all the ages to come, saying, "Sanctify them in the truth; Your word is truth" (John 17:17). Healing for our spiritual lameness—whether we need joy in affliction, greater fruitfulness, or growth in holiness—does not happen apart from the word of God.

You may get the word of God from sermons and Sunday school lessons.[7] You may get the word of Christ by listening to someone read the Bible while you are driving. You may get the word of Christ by reading and studying the Bible for yourself. The simple fact is this: If you want to get better, if you want the healing of Christ for your limping walk, you have to get _large_ doses of the Bible into your heart and mind. There are no shortcuts.

What do you need most? Your greatest need is not to figure out how Biblical prophecy lines up with yesterday's newscast. Your greatest need will never be satisfied by dwelling on the difficult, perplexing passages of the Bible. Limping Christians need large doses of the basic, saving message of the Bible. They need to get to know their

---

[7] You may download my sermons from the Internet at www.Godisbeautiful.com.

Father and their Savior and the Holy Spirit—not just in a feeling sort-of-way, but based on the foundational truths of the Bible. Read the gospels and the epistles; read the Psalms and Isaiah. Soak your soul in the most comforting, healing, challenging, strengthening, God-saturated passages you can find.

If you are limping along in your Christian life, Jesus is the only one who can heal you. He heals by His powerful word.

Jesus heals by His compassionate touch

Health care professionals increasingly collaborate electronically with their colleagues. Physicians and hospitals share patient records electronically or look up information on unusual diseases through the Internet. Pharmacists can check for drug interactions for their customers among all the medications different doctors have prescribed. During the Syrian civil war, specialists in the west used Skype to walk trauma doctors in Syria through complex operations on victims of the violence. Many patients may never know that their lives were saved by a doctor watching the procedure from thousands of miles away.

Jesus normally healed by the touch of His hands. During His ministry on earth, the

Lord rarely healed people at a distance. The gospel writers frequently mention that Jesus touched people to make them well. "While the sun was setting, all those who had any who were sick with various diseases brought them to Him; and laying His hands on each one of them, He was healing them" (Luke 4:40).

When Jesus touched people, He didn't just run through a crowd patting as many people as He could on the top of the head. His touch was personalized according to the needs of each suffering person. In a few cases, the gospels describe Jesus' touch in detail.

They brought to Him one who was deaf and spoke with difficulty, and they implored Him to lay His hand on him. Jesus took him aside from the crowd, by himself, and put His fingers into his ears, and after spitting, He touched his tongue with the saliva; and looking up to heaven with a deep sigh, He said to him, "Ephphatha!" that is, "Be opened!" And his ears were opened, and the impediment of his tongue was removed, and he began speaking plainly. And He gave them orders not to tell anyone; but the more He ordered them, the more widely they continued to proclaim it. They were utterly astonished, saying, "He has done all things well; He makes even the deaf to hear and the mute to speak" (Mark 7:32-37).

On at least three occasions, Jesus did heal at a distance, without even seeing the patient (John 4:46-53; Matthew 8:5-13; 15:21-28). These examples demonstrated that His healing power was not limited to His physical presence. He could touch people by His Holy Spirit when they were a few blocks or many miles away.

Jesus always healed by the touch of His Spirit. When John baptized Jesus, the Holy Spirit came on Him in the form of a dove (Luke 3:21-22). Then the Holy Spirit led Jesus into the wilderness to be tempted by the devil (Luke 4:2). After the temptation, "Jesus returned to Galilee in the power of the Spirit" (Luke 4:14). When He came to Nazareth, He explained His authority to preach and to heal by reading a prophecy from Isaiah 61.

The Spirit of the Lord is upon Me, because He anointed Me to preach the gospel to the poor. He has sent Me to proclaim release to the captives, and recovery of sight to the blind, to set free those who are oppressed, to proclaim the favorable year of the Lord (Luke 4:18-19).

Many people think that Jesus was able to do miracles because He was God, but Moses wasn't

God and he did miracles. Elijah wasn't God either, and he did miracles. Although Jesus was God, He did not do miracles using His own divine power. As the Messiah, the One anointed by the Holy Spirit, He did His miracles in the power of the Spirit. That is what the apostle Peter said when he preached to the Roman centurion, Cornelius: "You know of Jesus of Nazareth, how God anointed Him with the Holy Spirit and with power, and how He went about doing good and healing all who were oppressed by the devil, for God was with Him" (Acts 10:38).

Jesus always heals by the touch of His Spirit even when He is not physically present to touch the hurting with His hands. Many people, however, misunderstand how Jesus heals us by His Spirit because they separate the work of the Spirit from the word of God. The healing miracles of Christ accompanied the preaching of Christ, and most often, He spoke a personal word to the ones He healed. The healing ministry of the apostles also took place in conjunction with preaching the word of Christ.

People frequently separate the touch of the Spirit from the Bible, which is God's word to us. They want the Holy Spirit to be at work in their hearts, but they do not fill their hearts with the word of Christ. Jesus healed by His word and by

His Spirit. You can have His word without His Spirit, but you cannot have the touch of His Spirit for spiritual healing without His word. His word is in the Bible.

There is another problem related to neglect of the Bible. Some people think that the Spirit speaks with authority in mystical feelings. The problem is that once you separate the word of God from the Bible, you begin to think that your "spiritual feelings" must come from the Holy Spirit. "Spiritual feelings" apart from the clear teachings of the Bible are just ... feelings. They are not truly spiritual at all. Feelings that are not anchored in truth will lead you astray.

So how can you have the compassionate touch of Jesus to experience some measure of healing for your limping gait? Keep the word of Christ and the Spirit of Christ together. Immerse yourself in the word of God. Saturate your soul in what the Bible says about Christ and your heavenly Father and the Holy Spirit. As you read, think of yourself as though you were sitting at the feet of Jesus being taught by Him. Then ask the Lord to stretch out His hand through the power of the Spirit to heal you. Ask the Spirit to give you Bible-centered wisdom. Ask Him to give you courage to face difficult situations. Ask Him to give you strength to obey. Base these prayers on what you have just read in the Bible.

Jesus heals by His painful wounding

Nobody likes being hurt. Pain is bad. Nice feelings are good. Sometimes, however, we need pain in order to get well. When I developed cancer I felt no pain, but it needed to be cut out. Did I say, "Doctor, I don't like you. You hurt me. You are a bad man." No. I thanked my doctor for gouging around in my innards because I recognized that he wounded me only to heal me. We see the principle of a healing pain throughout the Bible.

> See now that I, I am He, and there is no god besides Me; it is I who put to death and give life. I have wounded and it is I who heal, and there is no one who can deliver from My hand (Deuteronomy 32:39).

> The Lord will strike Egypt, striking but healing; so they will return to the Lord, and He will respond to them and will heal them (Isaiah 19:22).

> Come, let us return to the Lord. For He has torn us, but He will heal us; He has wounded us, but He will bandage us. He will revive us after two days; He will raise us up on the third day, that we may live before Him. So let

us know, let us press on to know the Lord. His going forth is as certain as the dawn; and He will come to us like the rain, like the spring rain watering the earth (Hosea 6:1-3).

These are all Old Testament references, so we may wonder if Jesus ever wounded people before healing them? Wasn't He always just sympathetic and nice? No, sometimes He was firm or even angry.

Remember what Jesus told a rich young ruler after the young man claimed that he had obeyed God's law.

When Jesus heard this, He said to him, "One thing you still lack; sell all that you possess and distribute it to the poor, and you shall have treasure in heaven; and come, follow Me." But when he had heard these things, he became very sad, for he was extremely rich. And Jesus looked at him and said, "How hard it is for those who are wealthy to enter the kingdom of God! For it is easier for a camel to go through the eye of a needle than for a rich man to enter the kingdom of God." They who heard it said, "Then who can be saved?" But He said, "The things that are impossible with people are possible with God" (Luke 18:22-27).

Will this young man be in heaven? I don't know, but the last sentence gives me hope. Although he could not bring himself to set aside the burden of his wealth, God is able to change even the heart of a rich man. If this young man is in heaven, he will only be there because Jesus made him sorrowful first; Jesus had to wound him before he could be saved.

John 9 tells us about a man born blind. He was not born blind because of his parents' sin or because God looked ahead, saw that the man would sin, and punished him in advance. Jesus explained that he was born blind "so that the works of God might be displayed in him" (v. 3). Jesus gave him physical sight and spiritual sight on the same day, and the man gave consistent, determined testimony to Christ. God wounded him in preparation for healing him.

This principle that God wounds and God heals leads to some practical consequences for you when you are hurting.

Take comfort from His wounding. If you do not recognize the hand of God in your wounding, you may blame the devil or a bad man. The devil and bad people do not have any good intentions in mind when they hurt you. It is not very comforting to think you are at the mercy of a bad devil or a bad man.

On the other hand, perhaps you suppose you are hurting because of some totally random, accidental event. The dice were rolled, and they came out against you. It is not very comforting to think that blind fate has cursed you.

Perhaps you are limping because you feel helpless in the grip of sins you cannot master. That is not a comforting thought either.

Ah! What a difference it makes if a loving Father and a loving Savior have wounded you! Perhaps God has allowed the devil or a wicked person to torment you. He has only done it in order to push you closer to Christ.

The dice have not fallen out against you by accident for "The lot is cast into the lap, but its every decision is from the LORD" (Proverbs 16:33). Your Father and your Savior have prevented many harmful throws of the dice, so the afflictions that do come have been sent by Him to cause you to seek your joy in Jesus alone.

Those sins that seem impossible to resist—why hasn't the Lord removed them in answer to your prayer? He wants you to become strong as you learn to mortify them by the power of the Holy Spirit (Romans 8:12-13).[8] He normally will not take them away until you learn this vital lesson.

---

[8] For more on mortifying sin (putting sin to death) see the parable "Strangling the Serpent" on p. 125.

God allows some of your sins to afflict you and to make you miserable until you learn to rely on His word and His Spirit. It is more important to God that you learn to fill your heart with the word of Christ and to depend on the Spirit of Christ than that He magically cause your temptations to disappear.

Take comfort from God's wounding. The fact that Jesus heals by His painful wounding leads to a second principle.

Seek healing in His wounding. When we see that wounding sometimes is a necessary part of healing, we must not imagine that the healing will come automatically. We need to seek it diligently from the Lord.

Normally the cause of our sickness and the cause of our cure are different. We say, "A bug made me sick. The doctor gave me medicine to make me well. I broke my leg. The doctor set it and put it in a cast."

When we remember that the God who wounds is also the God who heals, we say: "God sent the bug. God will heal me. God broke my leg. God will heal it. Jesus is my Great Physician, I will go to Him and seek my healing."

And Levi gave a big reception for Him in his house; and there was a great crowd of tax collectors and other people who were reclining at the table with them. The Pharisees and their scribes began grumbling at His disciples, saying, "Why do you eat and drink with the tax collectors and sinners?" And Jesus answered and said to them, "It is not those who are well who need a physician, but those who are sick. I have not come to call the righteous but sinners to repentance" (Luke 5:29-32).

Jesus is the divine physician who loves to heal the burdened, the broken, and the battered. That is why He came, so we greatly err when imagine we will get well without seeking Him.

Limping Christian, Jesus is the only physician your spirit needs. What do I mean by this? Is there no place for medicine, for counselors, for books, and for seminars that address your problems? Surely, these things are gifts of God. Medicine for the mind is not different from medicine for the body, so a psychotropic drug may be a gift of God. God commands us to seek godly counsel and to learn His ways from each other, so a wise counselor is also a gift from God. How do these helps fit in with relying only on Jesus?

Think of it this way. In the Old Testament, God did not say it was wrong for Israel to have chariots. He said it was wrong for Israel to trust in chariots. "Some trust in chariots and some in horses, but we trust in the name of the LORD our God" (Psalm 20:7, ESV). Sometimes God gave victory when the king went out to fight with his chariots and his armed men. Sometimes God just killed the enemy soldiers without the army lifting a finger. In either case, God gave the victory.

Use whatever good helps God gives you, but do not trust in them. Place your trust in the Lord Jesus. Do not spend all your time and energy on pursuing these secondary helps so that you have no time to fill your heart with the word of Christ and seek the touch of His Spirit.

Let us not be like King Asa. For most of his reign, Asa followed the Lord, but in his old age, he strayed from the right path and imprisoned a prophet of God. Then, "In the thirty-ninth year of his reign Asa became diseased in his feet. His disease was severe, yet even in his disease he did not seek the LORD, but the physicians" (2 Chronicles 16:12). There was nothing wrong with consulting the physicians, but Asa used that as a replacement for trusting in the Lord.

No matter what other helpers you may find for your spiritual limping, do not place your confidence in them. Seek your healing from Him who has wounded you. I have seen people with an obvious spiritual disorder who run to their dysfunctional friends for sympathy and advice, but they will not seek their healing from Jesus in the ways that He has prescribed. To those ways, it is now time to turn.

CHAPTER 5
PHYSICAL THERAPY
FOR LIMPING CHRISTIANS

As I noted in the first chapter of this brief study, Hebrews 12 shows us several characteristics of limping Christians. Now it is time to look at the process by which God makes His limping children stronger.

> *All discipline for the moment seems not to be joyful, but sorrowful; yet to those who have been trained by it, afterwards it yields the peaceful fruit of righteousness. Therefore, strengthen the hands that are weak and the knees that are feeble, and make straight paths for your feet, so that the limb which is lame may not be put out of joint, but rather be healed (Hebrews 12:11-13).*

God has a plan for strengthening feeble knees and staggering, stumbling footsteps. It is called training or discipline. If we refuse to be trained, we won't get better.

After my wife's knee replacement, a physical therapist came to our home to work with her until she was ready for more aggressive treatment elsewhere. The therapist taught my daughter and me what to do with her in between visits. Our basic task was to torture her in order to improve her strength and range of motion. One day, the therapist told us about another client who had absolutely refused to do any exercises after his joint was replaced. He would not put himself through any pain in order to get better. So, of course, he did not get better. He even had to go back into surgery.

Our daughter-in-law provided us with the perfect description of the people we were paying to inflict that pain on my wife. She called them "physical terrorists."

How can you be trained and become strong through the painful things that are contributing to your spiritual limp? Before we look at the exercises Jesus prescribes to strengthen the limbs that are out of joint, we need to look at the things that help believers stick to those disciplines long enough to experience the good of them. Limping Christians need to trust the Great Physician and take their meds.

Trust your physician

Jesus is the only physician we need for our limping spirits. He is both our doctor and our physical therapist. He does it all. He may use secondary helps, but we trust in Him alone. What does it mean to trust the Great Physician when you are limping along through life?

Listen to His diagnosis of your disease. I have known more than one person who refused to go to the doctor even when they had potentially life-threatening physical problems. They did not want to hear what the doctor had to say. If we want to get well, we need to listen to Jesus' diagnosis of our disease. We must pray as David did,

> *Search me, O God, and know my heart;*
> *Try me and know my anxious thoughts;*
> *And see if there be any hurtful way in me,*
> *And lead me in the everlasting way*
> *(Psalm 139:23-24).*

On the surface, our problems may seem obvious. In most cases, however, the obvious issues are symptoms of a hidden spiritual illness. We need to allow the Lord Jesus to probe deeply and painfully into our motivations and desires, and we need to listen to what He says. The sins that trip up one person may seem to be quite different from the snares that entangle another, but they are often manifestations of the same deeper disease, the disease of pride.

➤ The greedy man wants to have more than others do. This is his way of feeling superior to them, but he has a hunger that can never be satisfied. He can never have enough to feel secure in his superiority to everybody else. (It is likewise with those who hunger for power and influence.) Pride likes to look down on others.

➢ The ordinary man bound up in pornography is not only addicted to sexual pleasure. He also wants to be obeyed and adored by the perfect woman. He wants to be a god to this imaginary woman. Pride wants to be worshiped by beauty.

➢ Perfectionists may be secretly pleased when they catch someone else making a mistake. They like to point out even small, insignificant errors to those who will appreciate their superior insight. Pride. (Of course, the perfectionist often suffers intense guilt from his own lack of perfection.)

➢ Resentment and anger toward God for life's unfair hardships derives from a sense that I have a right to something better. God should give me a better job or better health or better looks or a better family. Obviously not everyone can have these better things, but I should have them because I deserve them. Pride.

So look more deeply than the surface problems. Look at your reactions to the things that cause you to stumble. Ask the Great Physician to show you what He wants to heal. Trust involves listening to Him. You trust that He will not crush you by His diagnosis. He will not speak to you about your sins and shortcomings in order to gloat over you or to rub your nose in your failures. He does not want you to become overwhelmed by your guilt. He wants to point out the reason you are lame and stumbling about, in order to make you well. He loves you. Listen to Him.

Believe in your Physician's ability to heal. If you ask the average limping Christian, "Do you believe that Jesus can heal you?" he will say yes. That is the theologically correct answer. If you ask him about some specific thing he needs to do in obedience to the Lord, he may well answer, "I can't. I just can't." On one level that may be true. In his own strength, he cannot do what is asked of him. He seems, however, to mean more than that. He means, "I can't do this thing even with Jesus' help. This is just too difficult for Jesus to deal with." His "I can't" often means, "Jesus can't."

Dear brother or sister, Jesus *can* do all things. To a hundred-year-old man and his ninety-year-old wife, God said, "Is anything too difficult for the LORD? At the appointed time I will return to you, at this time next year, and Sarah will have a son" (Genesis 18:14). The birth of Isaac demonstrated that Yahweh is the God of the impossible. All of Scripture asserts the same truth.

Then Job answered the Lord and said, "I know that You can do all things, and that no purpose of Yours can be thwarted" (Job 42:1-2).

Whatever the Lord pleases, He does, in heaven and in earth, in the seas and in all deeps (Psalm 135:6).

Ah Lord God! Behold, You have made the heavens and the earth by Your great power and by Your outstretched arm! Nothing is too difficult for You (Jeremiah 32:17).

Because God can do all things, trusting your Great Physician, means that you say, "I can do all things through Him who strengthens me" (Philippians 4:13). If He asks you to swallow some bitter medicine in order to get well, your initial reaction might be, *"I can't."* When you look at Jesus and think of His almighty power, then by faith you must say, *"I can."*

Expect relief from your Physician's prayers because He is also your high priest. Every once in a while, I hear someone say, "My doctor said he prays for his patients." They say it with a sense of wonder and thankfulness. Perhaps many doctors pray for their patients, but it seems uncommon for them to say that they do. Jesus is the Great Physician who prays.

Expecting relief from the Lord is what it really means to trust in Him. This goes beyond listening to His diagnosis of your deep spiritual needs. It goes beyond trusting that He *can* do all things by His own mighty arm working in your circum-stances and in you. Expecting relief is a restful, hopeful trust. It is based on the clear teaching of the Bible that Jesus is a faithful, merciful high priest who constantly prays for you.

> *Therefore, since the children share in flesh and blood, He Himself likewise also partook of the same, that through death He might render powerless him who had the power of death, that is, the devil, and might free those who through fear of death were subject to slavery all their lives. For assuredly He does not give help to angels, but He gives help to the descendant of Abraham. Therefore, He had to be made like His brethren in all things, so that He might become a merciful and faithful high priest in things pertaining to God, to make propitiation for the sins of the people. For since He Himself was tempted in that which He has suffered, He is able to come to the aid of those who are tempted (Hebrews 2:14-18).*

Therefore, since we have a great high priest who has passed through the heavens, Jesus the Son of God, let us hold fast our confession. For we do not have a high priest who cannot sympathize with our weaknesses, but One who has been tempted in all things as we are, yet without sin. Therefore let us draw near with confidence to the throne of grace, so that we may receive mercy and find grace to help in time of need (Hebrews 4:14-16).

Jesus, your high priest promised to give you rest if you would come to Him and cast your burdens on Him. He understands your temptations because He was tempted just as we are. He will not be harsh to you. He will listen to your plea. He will present your urgent cries for help before the Father on the basis of His shed blood.

Come to Me, all who are weary and heavy-laden, and I will give you rest. Take My yoke upon you and learn from Me, for I am gentle and humble in heart, and you will find rest for your souls. For My yoke is easy and My burden is light (Matthew 11:28-30).

Oh, you whose souls are weary and crushed by a heavy burden, lean on this promise. Repeat it often to yourself. Expect relief from Jesus, but notice that the promise of rest comes with a condition. In order to find rest, you must take His yoke upon yourself. To take His yoke, means to shoulder the load He puts on you. It means that you obey Him and answer His call to discipleship.

Now let us suppose you are limping spiritually, and your trust in Christ is weak. You find yourself saying, "I can't stand it. I can't do what the Lord wants me to do. I can't bear my own load and His yoke as well. I don't really expect Jesus to give me relief. I just can't manage." This is a realistic problem for many people. Do not fear. Jesus does not expect you to bear both loads. He wants to trade loads with you, and His load is much lighter than the one you are carrying.

If you think you cannot carry His yoke, your Great Physician has medicine and some exercises to strengthen you for that task.

Take your medicine

Getting people to take their medicine must be one of the most frustrating problems doctors face. Some patients, when they are sick, take a few doses of the prescribed antibiotics. When they feel better, they stop. Those people should be taken to the public square and whipped because they are partly responsible for creating drug-resistant bacteria that harm the rest of the population. Others need to be on psychotropic drugs for their whole lives to even out wild mood swings, but I have known several who refuse to take their meds regularly. Then their families suffer.

It is even more serious and harder to understand when God's children refuse to take daily doses of the medicines their Great Physician has prepared and prescribed for them. These medicines are not foul tasting. They do not have unpleasant side effects. They are not harmfully addicting, but people neglect them anyway.

They are the sweetest, most comforting, most effective medicines in the world. You must take these medicines every day if you want to overcome your natural disbelief and learn to trust the Great Physician. If you do not take these medicines every day, your limp will get worse instead of better, and without these medicines the physical therapy your Physician has prescribed will not work.

Take daily doses of the blood of Christ for cleansing. When we first come to Christ, we are justified by His blood (Romans 5:9). As we mature in Christ, we never outgrow our need for His blood.

If we walk in the Light as He Himself is in the Light, we have fellowship with one another, and the blood of Jesus His Son cleanses us from all sin. If we say that we have no sin, we are deceiving ourselves and the truth is not in us. If we confess our sins, He is faithful and righteous to forgive us our sins and to cleanse us from all unrighteousness (1 John 1:7-9).

Perhaps you say, "I feel so guilty and worthless! There is no hope for me." OK, you *are* guilty and worthless; so am I. That is true. Now stop worrying about it. Get over it. Jesus has made you clean, and He keeps making you clean. Jesus has made you worth more than the entire universe. Heaven and earth will pass away, but you will not pass away because you belong to Him.

These verses ought to be written in gold on the tablets of your heart. Come to Jesus. His blood will cleanse you, not just once but day after day as often as you come to Him. When your trust in the Great Physician is weak and small because your sins rise up against you, plead the precious blood of Christ against your guilty conscience. You and I need this medicine every day.

Take daily doses of your union with Christ to experience freedom. God has united all believers to Jesus Christ. Scripture shows us several dimensions of that union. We have a natural union, a representative union, a voluntary union, and a spiritual union with

Christ.[9] God counts us as having died and risen with Christ. This union is more than a legal fiction, however. The Spirit of Christ in us really does unite us to Christ, who sits in heaven at the right hand of God. What does this mean for us? One thing it means is that we are no longer slaves of sin. After describing our union with Christ in His death and resurrection, the apostle Paul spells out one practical implication of that doctrine.

Even so consider yourselves to be dead to sin, but alive to God in Christ Jesus. Therefore do not let sin reign in your mortal body so that you obey its lusts, and do not go on presenting the members of your body to sin as instruments of unrighteousness; but present yourselves to God as those alive from the dead, and your members as instruments of righteousness to God. For sin shall not be master over you, for you are not under law but under grace. What then? Shall we sin because we are not under law but under grace? May it never be! Do you not know that when you present yourselves to someone as slaves for obedience, you are slaves of the one whom you obey, either of sin resulting in

---

[9] For an explanation of the different aspects of our union with Christ, see my book, *The Beauty of God for a Broken World,* chapter 6.

death, or of obedience resulting in right-eousness? But thanks be to God that though you were slaves of sin, you became obedient from the heart to that form of teaching to which you were committed, and having been freed from sin, you became slaves of righteousness (Romans 6:11-18).

Before you and I became Christians, we could not please God at all. Everything we did was a sin because we were living apart from God. Now we have been united to Christ in His death and resurrection. By His death and resurrection, Jesus has broken the chains of sin and death. We are no longer slaves to sin. We are free from its absolute domination over our lives. You may think that you cannot help sinning, but that is a lie that the devil tells you. You are not helpless. You have within you the mighty power of Christ's resurrection.

Why do people who are free from the enslavement of sin still act as if they were slaves? It is like this. After President Lincoln signed the Emancipation Proclamation, the slaves in America were free. They could leave their old masters if they wanted to, and many of them did. Many, however, did not. Slavery was all that they knew. They didn't know what to do with their freedom, so they stayed in bondage.

That happens to Christians as well. They have heard the proclamation of their freedom in Christ, but they do not truly believe it. They believe the lie of their former bondage. If you want healing from your limping spiritual condition, you need daily doses of this strong medicine: You have died and risen with Christ. You are free. As you begin to realize this wonderful truth in practice, you will grow in your ability to trust in the Great Physician.

Take daily doses of the Spirit of Christ for His purity.

For those who are according to the flesh set their minds on the things of the flesh, but those who are according to the Spirit, the things of the Spirit. For the mind set on the flesh is death, but the mind set on the Spirit is life and peace, because the mind set on the flesh is hostile toward God; for it does not subject itself to the law of God, for it is not even able to do so, and those who are in the flesh cannot please God. However, you are not in the flesh but in the Spirit, if indeed the Spirit of God dwells in you.... So then, brethren, we are under obligation, not to the flesh, to live according to the flesh—for if you are living according to the flesh, you must die; but if by the Spirit you are putting to death the deeds of the body, you will live (Romans 8:5-13).

The Holy Spirit is not just a doctrine (though the doctrine of the Spirit is vital). He is a Person. He is the Spirit of Christ and the Spirit of God the Father. Every holy desire that enters into your head and heart comes from Him.

How can you have a more personal and experiential knowledge of the Holy Spirit? Well, why not start by asking. "If you then, being evil, know how to give good gifts to your children, how much more will your heavenly Father give the Holy Spirit to those who ask Him" (Luke 11:13). Your Father loves to give you good things, and there is nothing better than a close, personal relationship with the Holy Spirit. Your Savior died to bring the Holy Spirit down from heaven into your heart. He knows that you cannot be holy on your own. Daily ask the Spirit to help you put your sinful desires to death. You will never do it perfectly until you get to heaven, but you will never do it at all without Him.

As you begin to develop an on-going, personal relationship with the Spirit of Christ, you will see that the Lord does help you when you call on Him. Your trust in the Lord will increase.

The title of this chapter is "Physical Therapy for Limping Christians." Now at last we come to the PT. You won't do your exercises if you don't trust your doctor, and you won't trust your doctor unless you have been looking at Him, seeing how trustworthy He is and how much He cares for you and does for you. Neither will you have strength for spiritual PT if you don't take your medicine.

Do your exercises

The exercises necessary for strengthening limbs that are out of joint are not anything secret or particularly difficult. People are always looking for something different from what the Great Physician has prescribed. They want God to do a special miracle for them so that they will not need to do the ordinary, daily stuff of the Christian life. If they have to do something, they want it to be an heroic sacrifice rather than the daily grind of disciplined exercise.

The way to become strong in body is to exercise regularly and diligently. Two of the young men in our church lift weights. Shortly after Christmas one year, they were talking (with some measure of disdain) about the people who make New Year's resolutions to exercise. For a little while, the gym is full of people who do not know how to use the equipment and who get in the way of those who have been lifting for years. However, in two or three months, most of the new people stop coming. Regular exercise is hard to keep up, but you cannot be strong without it. The same is true in the spiritual life.

Theologians have coined a term for the regular disciplines of the Christian life. They call them "the ordinary means of grace." They are *ordinary* because they are not shocking, new, or secret. They are just ordinary. They are *the means of grace* because they are the ways God graciously draws us closer to Himself. We need to stress the idea of God's *grace* because we are apt to think of these disciplines simply as duties we are supposed to perform if we want to be regarded as good Christians. The disciplines of the Christian life are not our way of improving ourselves. They are God's way of transforming us. Nevertheless, we must engage in them on a regular, disciplined basis.

Many people want to lose weight, but they are not willing to change their eating habits and exercise regularly. Many limping Christians want to walk vigorously without tiring, but they refuse to draw on the strength of Christ to do their spiritual exercises. That is the reason there are so many feeble knees and limbs that are out of joint in our churches. If you refuse to do your exercises, you will not get better. So what are these ordinary means of grace?

The gathered worship of the church is crucial for spiritual well-being. American individualists tend to assume that they can be nice, spiritual people all on their own. They do not need to be around a bunch of hypocrites at church in order to worship God. This is pure, foolish, unscriptural arrogance.

Let us hold fast the confession of our hope without wavering, for He who promised is faithful; and let us consider how to stimulate one another to love and good deeds, not forsaking our own assembling together, as is the habit of some, but encouraging one another; and all the more as you see the day drawing near (Hebrews 10:23-25).

This is very simple. It is very ordinary, yet it is a necessary discipline of the Christian life. Together we pray; together we praise God; together we hear the word of God proclaimed; together we take the Lord's Supper. Why do we do these things?

We do not do them to prove to others and ourselves how good we are. If you think you are proving your piety by going to church, you are only proving how snooty you are!

We do not do these things at church because they earn credit with God. They do not. Nor do they have an automatic tendency to make us holy.

We come together to sing, to pray, to hear God's word and to share in Christ's table because God meets with us here. God has appointed these ordinary things for our good. We need to sing and pray and hear and commune on a regular basis because we are so weak, so unholy, and so needy.

Therefore, when you are feeling miserable about yourself, that is the very time you need to come to the house of God. Do not stay away because you think you are not good enough to be in God's presence. You are, in fact, bad enough to need the presence of Christ in the midst of His people.

Perhaps at this point I should say a word about the Lord's Supper, or Communion. It is for baptized believers in Jesus Christ.[10] Beyond this basic criterion, who should receive the elements? If you are stubbornly holding on to some sin, and

---

[10] Baptism comes before communion because baptism celebrates our entrance into the church of Christ and communion celebrates our fellowship with Christ and His people in the church. The earliest description of Christian worship outside the New Testament is found in *The Teaching of the Twelve Apostles* (about A. D. 100). There we read, "But let no one eat or drink of this Eucharistic Thanksgiving [Communion], but they that have been baptized into the name of the Lord." Until fairly recently that was the practice of all branches of the church—Eastern Orthodox, Roman Catholic, and Protestant.

you have no intention of forsaking it, you should not share in the Supper. If, on the other hand, you are a struggling, limping Christian, if you are longing for mercy and strength, open your mouths to receive the bread and the cup. Open your heart to the one who gives Himself for your need in those very elements. The Supper is for sinners.

The encouragement of Christian fellowship is the second crucial means of grace. Hebrews 10 speaks of assembling together, and it speaks of encouraging one another. There are a great many *one-anothers* in the New Testament. We are to admonish one another, love one another, help one another, pray for one another, lift one another up from spiritual stumbles, and confess our sins to one another. Many sincere believers think that they should be able to manage the Christian life all on their own. They should be able to break sinful habits without any help. They should be able to walk consistently with the Lord and be filled with the Spirit all of the time—all on their own. In their eyes, the Christian life is just "Jesus and me in close relation."

We always need encouragement from each other beyond the experience of public worship. We need people to pray for us. As a pastor, I have often prayed for the sick, the suffering, and the sorrowing, but when I developed cancer (now cured), I was deeply moved when one of our deacons pulled me aside, laid his hands on me, and prayed for me.

If you are going through a stumbling, limping, hurting time in your life, you need a brother or sister with whom you can share your burdens and your sins. You need someone who is not afraid to rebuke or correct you, but who can do it with gentleness and love. This may seem very threatening. You wonder whom you can trust with the dark secrets of your soul. You may be afraid that the brother with whom you share your heart will look down on you or reject you. Obviously, you must choose your confidant well, but you need people in your life like Aaron and Hur, who held up the arms of Moses so that he could support Israel in its battle against the Amalekites (Exodus 17). Encouraging, strengthening fellowship is essential for becoming well and strong.

The practice of private devotions is the third ordinary means of grace. You cannot become strong and your limp will not be healed if you only depend on the gathered worship of the church and the fellowship of other believers. You and I need to have our own private times with God.

> *How blessed is the man who does not walk in*
>   *the counsel of the wicked,*
> *Nor stand in the path of sinners,*
> *Nor sit in the seat of scoffers!*
> *But his delight is in the law of the Lord,*
> *And in His law he meditates day and night.*
> *He will be like a tree firmly planted by*
>   *streams of water,*
> *Which yields its fruit in its season*
> *And its leaf does not wither;*
> *And in whatever he does, he prospers.*
> *The wicked are not so,*
> *But they are like chaff which the wind drives*
>   *away.*
> *Therefore the wicked will not stand in the*
>   *judgment,*
> *Nor sinners in the assembly of the righteous.*
> *For the Lord knows the way of the righteous,*
> *But the way of the wicked will perish*
> *(Psalm 1).*

Meditation on the word of God is the great, oft-neglected key to prospering spiritually. My favorite mental picture of meditation comes from the farm. Early in the morning, when a brown cow goes out and eats green grass to produce white milk, her food goes into the first part of her stomach. Later in the morning, you will see her lying down in the pasture chewing contentedly like a child with a big wad of gum. She has regurgitated her partially digested breakfast (called the cud) which she is now chewing for further processing in another part of her stomach. Meditation is like that.

First, we eat the word of God, perhaps by listening to it, but preferably by reading it for ourselves : "Your words were found and I ate them, and Your words became for me a joy and the delight of my heart; for I have been called by Your name, O LORD God of hosts" (Jeremiah 15:16). As part of our devotions, we need to spend some time mentally chewing on what we have read. It does us no good to gulp down a few bites of scriptural food before we rush out into our day. Later, when we have some quiet moments, we need to bring up the truth we have swallowed and chew it over again—just like that cow lying in the pasture in mid-morning. That is an essential part of thoroughly digesting the food of God's word.

By the way, I think it is a mistake for preachers of the word use their sermon study as a substitute for personal, devotional reading and meditation. I keep my private times with God and my Bible separate from my preparation for sermons. I do not want my devotions to become professionalized.

Silence is another essential aspect of our personal walk with God. It is certainly implied in meditation. When you meditate, you are listening to the Spirit of God speaking to you through

Scripture. I believe it is one of the ills of modern life that people constantly surround themselves with artificial noise. The television is on even if no one is watching it. Students must have music piped into their heads while they are doing homework. They may say they are multitasking, but numerous studies have shown that multi-tasking decreases efficiency, even though most multitaskers deny it. Our generation needs to learn to attend deeply and only to God. "Be still and know that I am God" (Psalm 46:10, ESV).

Prayer is the final stage of responding to what God has said to us. If you can turn what you have read into worship and praise or into heart-felt petitions for yourself or others, you are well on your way to learning how to pray. "God bless me and my family, Amen" may do for your nighttime prayer three seconds before your head hits the pillow, but chewing on and digesting the word of God will add depth and passion to your prayers.

Many Christians neglect private devotions whenever they are feeling spiritually down or especially sinful. Like Adam and Eve in the garden, they avoid God. They do not feel spiritually up to reading and praying. They feel guilty and unworthy to have fellowship with God. Of course, you are not worthy. Neither am I, even on my best day. The more unworthy we feel, the more important it is for us to seek God's face. What is the cleansing blood of Christ good for if it does not enable us sinners to come into the presence of God?

* * * *

I have described the gathered worship of God's people, Christian fellowship, and a private devotional life as spiritual exercises. What is their purpose? Unfortunately, some Christians view these things as if they were Boy Scout merit badges. If you do them well, then God and other people will recognize you as a Christian achiever. That is the wrong way of looking at things.

We do not practice these exercises to impress God. We do them because we trust our Physician, who has prescribed these disciplines for our good. We exercise, not to get a good grade in God's school, but because we believe that Jesus will use these practices to make us stronger.

The means of grace are not ends in themselves any more than the goal of physical therapy is doing the exercises. You can diligently practice all the means of grace and be an excellent Pharisee— proud of your achievement and disdainful of weaker brothers and sisters. The goal of spiritual exercises is to open you up to the grace of Christ. As His grace works in you, you can do what was impossible for you before. The goal is to enable you to walk without a limp so that you can love and obey your blessed Savior. The obedience that pleases God does not flow out our individual goodness and strength. It flows from the blood of Christ cleansing our sins. It flows from our union with Christ in His death and resurrection. It flows from the Spirit of Christ. We obey out of our weakness by His strength, and the goal of the disciplines is to teach us how to do that.

A Parable:
Strangling the Serpent

Death is an essential part of the Christian life in at least three ways.

First, there is a death that we share with Christ when we are united to Him by faith. *"I have been crucified with Christ"* (Galatians 2:20). This death is more fully described in Romans 6 where the "old man" is the old "I" that has died. (The "old man" is not the so-called "old sin nature," an error which has led many believers into despair.) Our union with Christ in His death means two things: first, the penalty of sin has been paid; second, we are free from the tyrannical domination of sin.

Second, there is a death that we have accomplished: *"Now those who belong to Christ Jesus have crucified the flesh with its passions and desires"* (Galatians 5:24). If all Christians have done this, it must have happened at conversion. What do we do at conversion that is like death? We repent of our sins; we turn from sin to Christ. Our lives take a new direction. Even though sin still nips at our heels, and causes us painful wounds, we are headed toward our

Savior. We have turned our back on our old way of life.

Third, there is a daily death that is our constant battle. Jesus said that we must take up our crosses daily in order to follow Him (Luke 9:23). "So then, brethren, we are under obligation, not to the flesh, to live according to the flesh—for if you are living according to the flesh, you must die; but if by the Spirit you are putting to death the deeds of the body, you will live" (Romans 8:12-13).

This third kind of death is my subject for the next few paragraphs. Note the present tense of the verbs, *"are living"* and *"are putting to death."* Unfortunately, most of the popular English translations do not indicate the progressive action of the verbs that is so clear in the *New American Standard Bible*. They simply say, *"if you put to death the deeds of the body."* This may imply, as one man said to me, "If you put a sin to death, isn't it dead and gone?" As a corrective to that notion, I offer a parable.

Sin is like a boa constrictor that is squeezing the life out of you. Some people think that killing sin is like chopping off the head of the snake with a machete. It is dead. It can't bother you anymore. Here is a better picture.

The boa constrictor is trying to squeeze the life out of you. You have your hands around its neck, but you are not strong enough to save yourself, so you cry out to the Holy Spirit to help you. Then the invisible hands of God are placed over your hands, and you begin to strangle that snake. The Spirit doesn't strangle the snake apart from your hands being on its neck. He only does it through your hands. Finally, it goes limp, so you let go and push it off from you.

Now you are walking down the trail glad and happy, but that snake is not dead. It begins to recover, and it slithers along the trail behind you and up into a tree. Then it drops down on top of you and begins to choke you again. It is not as strong as it was before because it feels the effects of being strangled, but it is still stronger than you are. You would surely die and become its prey except that you cry out to the Holy Spirit who puts His hands over yours so that you can strangle the snake again.

This process happens repeatedly. Each time you cry out for the Spirit's help, the snake becomes a little weaker. It is not killed all at once, but you are gradually putting it to death by the help of the Spirit. There may come a day when that particular sin truly is dead in your life, but you can never let your guard down, and it is not the only snake in the jungle.

You cannot put sin to death by yourself, and the Spirit will not do it without you, but with His hands covering your hands you can strangle the snake so that it dies a bit at a time. That is what it means to be progressively putting sin to death by the Spirit. If your besetting sin does not die completely in this life (and few things do), sin and Satan will be utterly crushed under your feet when the Spirit raises your body to share in the glorious resurrection of Christ (Romans 8:9-11; Romans 16:20).

CHAPTER 6
RESURRECTION
FOR LIMPING CHRISTIANS

The grandchildren are all at Grandpa's house swimming in his pool. Grandpa cups his hands around his mouth and shouts to get the attention of all the squealing, laughing children. "I want everybody to move to the edge of the pool and close your eyes. Keep your eyes shut." When Grandpa is satisfied that no one is peeking, he tosses several handfuls of quarters into various parts of the pool. "When I say, 'Go' you may open your eyes and dive for quarters. You may keep all that you bring up." So the children dive eagerly after the coins. The older ones leave a few on purpose for the younger children, and everyone is happy. (He is a very generous Grandpa. I would have thrown pennies.)

The point I want to make from this parable is that the children can only bring up the coins that they pick up from the bottom of the pool. If no one picks up the quarter under the ladder, it just stays there.

In the same way, Jesus was only able to take up to God what He picked up when He dove down into this world. Anything He did not pick up, He could not take up. That is a very important principle. Throughout church history, people keep trying to limit the humanity of Christ in some way, but if He did not take on our whole human nature, then when He rose from the grave and ascended to heaven, He left part of our humanity behind at the bottom of the pool. The part He left behind was not raised with Him up to heaven.

In the second and third centuries after Christ, some heretics suggested that Jesus did not have a real human body. I have read a Gnostic text that describes Jesus walking along the seashore and leaving no footprints in the sand. That heresy has not died out even to this day. My children were once given a Bible storybook that pictured the risen Christ walking with two of His disciples. The disciples had feet, but Jesus didn't. He just floated along.

In the early church, after the New Testament, other heretics said that Jesus had a human body and a human soul, but not a human spirit. They said the Holy Spirit took the place of His human spirit. This heresy is also still alive. I met someone several years ago who described Jesus in this way. I think he picked up the idea from one of the health and wealth preachers on television.

If there was any part of our humanity that Jesus did not possess, for example our human spirit, that is a part He could not save. A famous early Christian teacher said it this way:

> For that which He has not assumed[11] He has not healed; but that which is united to His Godhead is also saved. If only half Adam fell, then that which Christ assumes and saves may be half also; but if the whole of his nature fell, it must be united to the whole nature of Him that was begotten, and so be saved as a whole (Gregory of Nazianzus, Epistle 101).[12]

Since Jesus took on our whole human nature, His resurrection will raise us—finally made whole—unto God.

The risen Jesus gives us life

In my little parable, the children came up with coins in their hands, and I compared the coins to the whole of our human nature that Jesus picked up when He came to earth. You might say to me, "Well, it is very nice that Jesus took our human nature back to heaven, but what good has that done me? He left me at the bottom of the pool." Ah, but that is not quite the whole story. Suppose

---

[11] Assumed = taken on to Himself.
[12] Gregory died AD 389.

one of the children had attached a string to one of the coins (perhaps with a huge wad of bubble gum). Then he could have pulled that coin up by the string. Jesus has tied an unbreakable string between Himself and the people He saves. Our bodies and souls are tied to the body and soul of Jesus by the Holy Spirit, and by the Spirit, Jesus will pull us up to where He is.

> *However, you are not in the flesh but in the Spirit, if indeed the Spirit of God dwells in you. But if anyone does not have the Spirit of Christ, he does not belong to Him. If Christ is in you, though the body is dead because of sin, yet the [human] spirit is alive because of righteousness. But if the Spirit of Him who raised Jesus from the dead dwells in you, He who raised Christ Jesus from the dead will also give life to your mortal bodies through His Spirit who dwells in you.... The Spirit Himself testifies with our spirit that we are children of God, and if children, heirs also, heirs of God and fellow heirs with Christ, if indeed we suffer with Him so that we may also be glorified with Him. For I consider that the sufferings of this present time are not worthy to be compared with the glory that is to be revealed to us (Romans 8:9-18).*

If you belong to Jesus, the Spirit of Christ lives in you, and He gives you life. Oh, I hope that none of you reading this book will put it down without receiving the crucified, risen Christ as your own Lord and Savior. When you have Him, you have life. Without Him, you have only death.

Jesus gives eternal life to our spirits. "If Christ is in you, though the body is dead because of sin, yet the spirit is alive because of righteousness" (v. 10).

Christ lives in us by His Spirit. The life He gives us is His very own life, which is eternal. Every child of God has the life of God united to his human spirit. Since the Holy Spirit ties your human spirit to the human spirit of Jesus, your spirit is already raised up to God. You and I are already seated with Christ in the heavenly places (Ephesians 2:6).

The Bible uses a number of different words to describe the non-physical part of our human nature: *heart, kidneys, breath, soul, spirit, mind*, and *bowels* are common ones. These words don't always appear in English versions because the translators are apt to use "heart" for several of them. They are not separate parts of our non-physical nature. They describe different functions of our whole inner identity. When the Bible says that our spirits are alive, it does not mean our spirits are alive, but our souls are dead. It means the whole invisible part of us is alive—the part of us that thinks, loves, sorrows, remembers, and rejoices. Our inner self is alive because the Spirit of God lives in us. We have eternal life now, the life of God Himself.

Jesus gives resurrection life to our bodies. When believers die, their disembodied spirits go to be with the Lord, and their bodies go back into the dust from which they came (2 Corinthians 5:1-8; Revelation 6:9-11). When the risen Lord Jesus comes again, He will pull your body up from the grave, transforming it at the same time into the likeness of the glorious body He now has in heaven (1 Corinthians 15:35-58; Philippians 3:20-21). He will put your spirit and your body back together, so you will be whole. Then your spirit and your body will be with Him forever. Jesus came down to the bottom of the pool to take on a human spirit and a human body so that He could redeem our bodies and spirits and not leave any part of us behind.

How will Christ pull us up to Himself? Remember the coin that was pulled up from the bottom of the pool by a string stuck to it? What is the unbreakable cord that ties us to Jesus? The Holy Spirit is that cord. The body and human spirit of Jesus are in heaven, but the Holy Spirit unites our bodies and spirits to the human body and human spirit of Jesus.

Now God has not only raised the Lord, but will also raise us up through His power. Do you not know that your bodies are members of Christ? ...But the one who joins himself to the Lord is one spirit with Him.... Or do you not know that your body is a temple of the Holy Spirit who is in you, whom you have from God, and that you are not your own (1 Corinthians 6:14-19)?

When He returns in the clouds of divine glory, Jesus will pull us up by the Holy Spirit into the presence of God. Since Jesus took on our whole human nature, His resurrection will raise us—finally made whole—into the presence of God.

The risen Jesus heals our limps

Jesus partially heals our limping condition when we learn to rest in Him. He will bring complete healing when He lifts us to glory. How will He do that? How is our healing related to His complete humanity?

When the resurrected Jesus appeared the second time to His apostles, He invited Thomas to touch with his finger the nail holes in His hand and to put his hand into the spear wound in His side (John 20:27). The risen Christ still bore the wounds of His crucifixion.

Even now in heaven, the Lord Jesus carries those marks.

> *And I saw between the throne (with the four living creatures) and the elders a Lamb standing, as if slain, having seven horns and seven eyes, which are the seven Spirits of God, sent out into all the earth (Revelation 5:6).*

Of course, John saw the Lamb in a vision. Jesus does not actually look like a lamb any more than He literally has a sword sticking out of His mouth as Revelation 1 and 19 describe Him. Nevertheless, these vivid visions of Christ are not arbitrary images. They have meaning, and the meaning of the slain Lamb is that Jesus took His wounds with Him to heaven. Even though His human body is now wonderfully powerful and glorious, He is a wounded Savior, but His wounds are not now ugly. They are a glorious testimony to His grace and love.

All of the burdens Jesus bore on earth, all of His trials, and all of His troubles went up to heaven with Him so that He could transform them into heavenly majesty. Because we are tied to Him by His Spirit, He bore our trials and troubles as well as His own, and He carried them up to heaven in order to transform them into beauty and glory. We get some sense of what Jesus bore and took to heaven in Isaiah 53. This amazing prophecy of Jesus' death and resurrection was written 700 years before He was born.

Jesus bore our sins to make us holy.

But He was pierced through for our transgressions, He was crushed for our iniquities; the chastening for our well-being fell upon Him, and by His scourging we are healed. All of us like sheep have gone astray, each of us has turned to his own way; but the Lord has caused the iniquity of us all to fall on Him (Isaiah 53:5-6).

As a result of the anguish of His soul, He will see it and be satisfied; by His knowledge the Righteous One, My Servant, will justify the many, as He will bear their iniquities. Therefore, I will allot Him a portion with the great, and He will divide the booty with the strong; because He poured out Himself to death, and was numbered with the transgressors; yet He Himself bore the sin of many, and interceded for the transgressors (Isaiah 53:11-12).

Jesus bore our sins, variously described as our transgressions and iniquities. The first result of Jesus bearing our sins is that God forgives all who trust in Jesus. He counts us righteous. That is what verse 12 means when it says, "My Servant will justify many." If you belong to Christ, you are justified right now. You are forgiven. You are righteous in God's sight.

But there is more. Though Jesus cast off the dreadful weight of our sins when He burst forth from the tomb, He still carries the knowledge of our sins. He knows how your sins trip you up and make you stumble. He knows how frustrated you are when you try, and fail, to break free of sinful habits. You are tied to Him by an unbreakable cord, so He feels your falls and your failures. In that sense, He still bears your sins.

What is He going to do about them? He is working now in you by His Spirit to help you fight against your sins. Later on, when He raises you by His Spirit into glory He will make you and me holy. We will love righteousness. We will be thrilled by goodness. We will be passionate about purity. Sin will become despicable in our eyes, and we will wonder how we ever found it desirable.

When you are limping along under the burden of your sins, look up to heaven where Jesus sits at the right hand of the Father. By and by, He will draw you up, body and soul, to sit by His side in holiness. That is your hope. That is your confidence.

Jesus bore our sorrows to give us joy.

He was despised and forsaken of men, a man of sorrows and acquainted with grief; and like one from whom men hide their face He was despised, and we did not esteem Him. Surely our griefs He Himself bore, and our sorrows He carried; yet we ourselves esteemed Him stricken, smitten of God, and afflicted (Isaiah 53:3-4).

The words *sorrows* and *griefs* may refer to physical pains and sickness or to emotional and spiritual suffering. In the case of Christ, both were involved because verse 11 speaks of "the anguish of His soul."

Jesus bore **our** sorrows. He bore **our** griefs. His soul was in anguish because of **us**. Sorrow and grief come into our lives because we are sinners living in a sin-damaged world. We get some sense of Jesus' sorrow and grief from three incidents in the gospels.

The first is when Jesus wept and was deeply troubled at the tomb of His friend Lazarus (John 11:33-38). He wept even though He was planning to raise Lazarus from the dead. He wept because He felt very deeply the grief of Lazarus's sisters and friends. He wept because He knows the pains of death.

The second is when Jesus wept over Jerusalem. He was riding on the colt of a donkey. The people were cheering wildly, waving palm branches and laying their coats down in front of the donkey. When Jesus came to the Mount of Olives and looked down on the city, He stopped and wept over the destruction that would come about 37 years later (Luke 19:41-44). The tears of Jesus must have seemed very strange to those cheering pilgrims, but they did not see the disaster ahead as He did.

Our third insight into the grief and sorrow of Jesus comes on the night before His crucifixion when Jesus cried out, "Father, if You are willing, remove this cup from Me; yet not My will, but Yours be done" (Luke 22:42). Hebrews 5:7 tells us that He offered up His prayer "with loud crying and tears." Jesus dreaded going to the cross. He was a "man of sorrows and acquainted with grief."

Because you are united to Jesus by the unbreakable bond of the Holy Spirit, He bears your sorrows and your griefs even now. Your losses, the burdens that weigh you down, your disappointments, and the sudden blows of life that knock you off your feet—Jesus bears those along with you.

What is He going to do about them? Well, right now He wants to give you a quality of peace that the world knows nothing about. He wants to give you rest. O brother, o sister lay your burdens on Jesus and seek His rest. He is more eager to give you rest than you are able to believe in that rest.

Present rest is not all the risen Jesus has for you. When Jesus draws you up to where He is, He will turn every sorrow into joy. He will turn your mourning into dancing; He will remove the rough, itchy sackcloth of your grief to fill you with gladness (Psalm 30:5, 11-12).

When you are limping along because of all the hard stones with which the world has bruised you, when sorrow is your daily food, look up where Jesus sits at the right hand of the Father. By and by, He will draw you up to sit beside Himself in boundless joy.

Jesus bears our suffering to share His glory. Isaiah 53 describes the physical, emotional, and spiritual suffering of our Savior, ending in His death as a sacrifice for our sins. The chapter closes with this remarkable verse.

Therefore, I will allot Him a portion with the great, and He will divide the booty with the strong; because He poured out Himself to death, and was numbered with the transgressors; yet He Himself bore the sin of many, and interceded for the transgressors (Isaiah 53:12).

After Jesus died for our sins, God allotted Him a portion with the great. How can you give a dead person a reward among the living? Only by raising Him from the dead. After His resurrection, Jesus told His disciples, "All authority has been given to me in heaven and on earth" (Matthew 28:18).

Isaiah 53:12 goes on to say, *"And He will divide the booty with the strong."* He will share with the strong the glory that the Father has given Him. With whom will Jesus share the treasure He won by His death and resurrection? He will share it with us. We are the strong ones, not by our own strength, but by the power of the Holy Spirit.

For you have not received a spirit of slavery leading to fear again, but you have received a spirit of adoption as sons by which we cry out, "Abba! Father!" The Spirit Himself testifies with our spirit that we are children of God, and if children, heirs also, heirs of God and fellow heirs with Christ, if indeed we suffer with Him so that we may also be glorified with Him (Romans 8:15-17).

We suffer with Him. Yes, but He also suffers with us. We cannot make Jesus suffer, but He chooses to share our sufferings in order to share with us His eternal glory.

Limping brother or sister, your present sufferings are a painful, but necessary prelude to unimaginable glory. Jesus rose from a dark and dismal grave into the glorious light of heaven. If you are in a dark and dismal place, do not take that as the final word in your story. By His Spirit, Jesus will draw you up out of that awful place to where He sits in glory. Remember that. Rest in that. Look forward to that.

The night before His crucifixion, Jesus prayed that you and I would share in His glory, and it is impossible that the Father would not answer His Son's prayer.

> The glory which You have given Me I have given to them, that they may be one, just as We are one; I in them and You in Me, that they may be perfected in unity, so that the world may know that You sent Me, and loved them, even as You have loved Me. Father, I desire that they also, whom You have given Me, be with Me where I am, so that they may see My glory which You have given Me, for You loved Me before the foundation of the world (John 17:22-24).

The glory that lies ahead is something so amazing that we cannot now imagine what it means. We can state it, but we cannot comprehend it. It is **Union with the Triune God.**

Our eternal destiny is not just to live in a beautiful place where there is no sorrow or pain. Our eternal destiny is not just to be with Grandma and the rest of our saved loved ones. Our eternal destiny is union with the Triune God.

Some branches of Hinduism imagine that your little drop of water will be swallowed up in the great ocean of Being. You will cease to exist as an individual. That is not the kind of union with God that the Bible promises.

We will be one with God and yet separate from Him. God's glory will be in us and upon us, but we will look at the glory of Jesus Christ and know Him to be infinitely above us. This miracle will come about because God took on Himself a complete human nature to bear our sins, our sorrows, and our suffering, and to lift us up into union with Himself.

When you are limping along day by day, slogging through the deep mud of this life, remember where the risen Christ is taking you. "Lift up your head, for your redemption draweth nigh" (Luke 21:28, KJV).

If you do not belong to Christ, He will not raise you to holiness, joy and glory. Your lot is as unimaginably terrifying as the lot of the saved is glorious. Will you not today repent of your sin and receive your Savior? I pray that you will.

A Parable: Millie

Once upon a time, a good Christian couple had three children. The oldest was Carl. He was very smart. He always got straight A's on his report card. His parents were very proud of him. The youngest child was Cassandra. She was a beautiful girl with a voice like an angel's. Even when she was three years old, she could carry a tune, and by the time she was twelve, she was giving concerts in area churches. Her parents were very proud of her. The middle child was just Millie, plain, ordinary Millie. She struggled in school; her face and figure were a little lumpy and lop-sided, and she had no special talents. She was awkward in social settings because she had trouble saying what she meant. Sometimes her words came out all tangled up, and people looked at her in a funny way. Her brother and her sister were always a little bit embarrassed to be around her. After graduation from high school, she found work in a small factory. She never married.

Carl became a missionary. He and his wife went to an unreached tribe in Papua New Guinea. They reduced the language of the tribe to writing and several hundred tribes' people came to the Lord Jesus. Whenever Carl was home on furlough, he went to visit Millie for a couple of hours—seldom longer. She was thrilled to see him, and she understood why he could not spend more time with her. After all, he had so many other supporters and important people to contact.

Cassandra became a world-famous singer. In her concerts, she always gave glory to the Lord Jesus Christ. Unlike many famous performers, she was faithful to her husband, and she took good care of her children. Millie followed her sister's career with great pride. She kept a scrapbook of newspaper clippings and photos, and she bought every tape and CD her sister recorded. She did not see Cassandra very often, but sometimes she was invited for Christmas dinner. That meant a ten-hour bus ride for Millie each way for a one-day visit, but she didn't mind in the least. Once, Cassandra invited her to a nearby concert. Millie had a seat in the very front row, but of course Cassandra did not introduce her to the crowd.

It came to pass that Carl, Millie and Cassandra all died on the same day and arrived at the pearly gates at the same time. Carl stepped up to the gates first. After all, he had been a successful missionary. Cassandra stood behind him. Last of all was Millie. The gates began to swing open, and Saint Peter was about to come out and welcome the new arrivals when the Lord called out from behind him. "Not this time, Peter. I'll welcome them Myself."

The Lord Himself appeared at the gate and said, "Millie, please come to the front of the line. You are the last who must be the first today."

"Wh. . . Wh. . . Why me?" stammered Millie.

The Lord put His arm around Millie as He spoke to her brother and sister. "Carl and Cassandra, I love you and I am pleased to welcome you into heaven today, but Millie shall come in first. She loved you both with all of her heart, not only because you were her brother and sister but because you were serving Me.

"Carl, you did truly value the little bit of money she sent you every month, but did you know that in order to send it she bought all of her clothes at the Good Will. She turned the heat in her apartment down to 62 degrees in the winter, and sometimes she went hungry. Cassandra, you had very little time for your sister, but she had much time for you. She often prayed more for you in a day than you spent talking with her in a year. Carl and Cassandra, I blessed your work because of her prayers. You labored much, but she loved much. Therefore, she will come in today ahead of you. What matters in the end is not how much you have done, but how well you have loved.

SCRIPTURE FOR LIMPING SEASONS

In your time of need, I encourage you to read a few of these passages repeatedly throughout the day. Do not say to yourself, "OK, I already know what that verse says. What good is it doing me?" Knowing what a passage says is not enough. You must mull it over in your mind; you must hold it in your heart; you must digest it so that it becomes a part of you. That is the meaning of meditation (Psalm 1). If a passage of Scripture does not live within you, it will do you no good. My wife has printed out a number of these and put them under her clear desk-protector in order to see them often. You might also find a place to post the ones that are most meaningful to you.

When your faith is small

> Matthew 14:22-33
> Mark 9:24 (see vv. 17-29)
> Luke 17:5-6

When you have sinned deeply

> Psalm 32
> Psalm 51
> Psalm 103:8-13
> Luke 7:36-50
> 1 Timothy 1:12-17

When you are overwhelmed

Psalm 42:7 (read the whole psalm)

Psalm 66:8-12

Isaiah 43:1-4

When you are inadequate

2 Chronicles 20:14-17

Psalm 20:6-7

2 Corinthians 2:14-16 and 3:4-6

When you are anxious

Isaiah 41:10

Matthew 6:25-34

Philippians 4:4-13, 19

When you are weary

Isaiah 40:28-31

Jeremiah 31:25

Matthew 11:28-30

When your pride needs to be humbled

Isaiah 57:15

Luke 14:7-14

1 Peter 5:5-9

When you are tempted to complain about trials

Romans 5:1-5

James 1:2-4, 12

1 Peter 1:3-9

When you need peace
Isaiah 26:3-4

John 14:27

John 16:33

When you need the power of Christ
2 Corinthians 4:7-11

2 Corinthians 12:9-10

When you need a refuge
Psalm 27:1-5, 13-14

Psalm 46:1, 10-11

Psalm 62:1-2, 5-8

ABOUT THE AUTHOR

John K. LaShell has a BA from Moody Bible Institute, an MA from Talbot Theological Seminary in LaMirada, California, and a PhD from Westminster Seminary in Philadelphia. He has served churches in Wisconsin, Montana, and Pennsylvania. For seven years, he taught humanities as an adjunct professor at a branch campus of Penn State. He has been the pastor of Grace Community Church in Allentown, Pennsylvania, for the past 20 years.

His wife and helpmeet, Heather, is a Registered Nurse. They have two children and four grandchildren. Heather and John ("Hither and Yon") enjoy walking, canoeing, and traveling together.

Dr. LaShell is the author of one previous book, *The Beauty of God for a Broken World: Reflections on the Goodness of the God of the Bible*, published by CLCPublications in 2010. Information about that book, audio sermons, contact information, and a few other tidbits may be found at **www.Godisbeautiful.com**. Outlines of other books in preparation may be found on the website as well.

Made in the USA
Columbia, SC
04 February 2021